katharine kaye mcmillan

CHRISTMAS

at Designers' Homes Across America

patricia hart mcmillan

4880 Lower Valley Road • Atglen, PA 19310

OTHER SCHIFFER BOOKS BY THE AUTHORS:
Christmas at America's Landmark Houses
ISBN 978-0-7643-4996-6

Christmas at Historic Houses, Revised 2nd Edition
ISBN 978-0-7643-4690-3

OTHER SCHIFFER BOOKS ON RELATED SUBJECTS:
Christmas 1960 to the Present: A Collector's Guide to Decorations and Customs
 ISBN 978-0-7643-2245-7

Christmas Plates: from Royal Copenhagen and Bing & Grondahl,
ISBN 978-0-7643-2089-7

Designed by Danielle D. Farmer
Cover design by Danielle D. Farmer
Cover: Interior design by Shayla Copas, photo by Janet Warlick
Type set in Walbaum MT/Carpenter

ISBN: 978-0-7643-5163-1
Printed in China

Published by Schiffer Publishing, Ltd.
4880 Lower Valley Road
Atglen, PA 19310
Phone: (610) 593-1777; Fax: (610) 593-2002
E-mail: Info@schifferbooks.com
Web: www.schifferbooks.com

*For our complete selection of fine books on this and related subjects, please
visit our website at www.schifferbooks.com. You may also write for a free
catalog.*

*Schiffer Publishing's titles are available at special discounts for bulk
purchases for sales promotions or premiums. Special editions, including
personalized covers, corporate imprints, and excerpts, can be created
in large quantities for special needs. For more information, contact the
publisher.*

*We are always looking for people to write books on new and related
subjects. If you have an idea for a book, please contact us at proposals@
schifferbooks.com.*

Dedicated to

Jesus, the Christ

*For God so loved the world, that he gave his only
begotten Son, that whosoever believeth in
him should not perish, but have everlasting life.*

—John 3.16, KJV

CONTENTS

FOREWORD

Viewing Christmas

A SMALL CONFESSION: If a woman can be a Peeping Tom, then I am one. *But only at Christmastime.* When tree lights begin to sparkle inside my neighbors' homes, I can't resist looking in on their holidays, their ways of dressing up for the most colorful and joyous season of the year.

Standing outside in the delicious, deep dark blue of a cold mid-winter evening, I can feel the warmth glowing through windows deliberately left uncovered, the lights from each house I pass flowing out to illuminate the universal message of peace and love.

Christmas has always been a magical time for me. My childhood Christmases remain a colorful blur of chubby tree lights and bubble lights (tiny LEDs were far in the future), faux snow that came in boxes to blizzard the tiny landscapes we created under the tree, and tinsel icicles that had to be draped, one-by-painstaking-one, from only the tips of the tree branches.

Christmas then was also about chocolate-covered cherries, walnuts, and the occasional sip of grown-ups' eggnog! My Christmases today still smell of oranges—Santa left one in the toe of our stockings, puzzling me because we had oranges all year long. My equally puzzled children also got oranges in their stockings a generation later.

Tradition, tradition! Every family has theirs. Every one of us plans and decorates for Christmas in our own special way—I know that from secretly peeping into my neighbors' homes.

Or perhaps it wasn't so secret. Perhaps Patricia Hart McMillan and I have been colleagues and friends for so long that she guessed my holiday voyeur habit. She and daughter Katharine might have written this inspired book just for me. No more pressing my nose against an icy windowpane; Pat and Kat take us all up the steps, through the open front door, and right inside some of the most remarkable homes in America . . . into the private spaces of top design talents all across the country.

Bring your notebook. New decorating ideas are everywhere for the lifting. Traditional. Eccentric. Witty. Highly personal. This is how the uber-creative festoon their own rooms at Christmas. Usually, only family and friends are invited in, but turn the page and join the party.

There may even be some grown-up eggnog!

—Rose Bennett Gilbert, syndicated design columnist

ACKNOWLEDGMENTS

We thank publisher Pete Schiffer, who believed that it is important to document interiors by leading designers who lavish their talents on preparing their homes to celebrate the Christmas season. We thank the designers who opened their homes and hearts to us. We salute your talent and admire your generous spirits. We wish you many more very merry Christmases.

Photograph by David Strahan

INTRODUCTION

AT HOME: Designers Coast to Coast

For this one special time of year, designers transform their homes into winter wonderlands. Christmas trees replete with fancy ornaments and bright garlands, twinkling lights, and glittering tinsel delight their family and friends. The work is a labor of love, done purely for the joy of seeing children's faces beam with happiness and grown-ups glow with good cheer. Designers do not often open their homes to the public, but here they share their visions for the holiday.

Each designer featured has a singular approach to decorating for the season. We glimpse the stately New York home of Christopher Radko, who has been credited with single-handedly reviving interest in Victorian and retro Christmas ornaments. Event planner Gary Mullis's own home features thousands of Radko ornaments. In contrast to Radko, designer and antiques dealer Mary Helen McCoy is all about traditional, understated elegance. Roses, the ancient symbol of Jesus, are her holiday flower of choice—don't look for poinsettias there!

A tremendous range exists between these extremes. Cecil Hayes weaves elements of Florida—seashells and butterflies—into her tapestry of holiday decorating. So do Lance Jackson and David Ecton, with their Palm Beach scheme. Memories of Christmas Past define Denise McGaha's holiday look, and antiques dealer Jenny Lunney has an eye for the eclectic.

Every designer uses color differently, too. Brilliant whites and metallic hues grace the home of DesAnn Collins, while orange and turquoise dominate Palm Beach designer Keith Carrington's interior. The designers featured here are spread out across the US and are easily found online through their websites, blogs, and social media sites. We hope that in these pages you, dear reader, will find inspiration for celebrating Christmas in style—*your* style.

—Katharine Kaye McMillan

It is a "blue Christmas" in this exuberantly lemon-hued parlor.

At home with

Christopher Radko

Irvington, New York

The *New York Times* dubbed Christopher Radko the Czar of Christmas Present— all because he reignited the love that millions have for vintage Christmas tree ornaments. Says Radko, "My ornaments grace the trees of stars including Bruce Springsteen, Dolly Parton, Elton John, Al Pacino, Mikhail Baryshnikov, Oprah Winfrey, Whoopi Goldberg, Ben Affleck, Julie Andrews, Robert De Niro, Angelina Jolie, Colin Farrell, Katy Perry, Scarlett Johansson, Hugh Jackman, and Beyonce. Barbra Streisand convinced me to start making Hanukkah ornaments, which I gladly did. In my earlier years, Hollywood collectors of my ornaments included Katharine Hepburn, Gregory Peck, Lauren Bacall, Jimmy Stewart, and Elizabeth Taylor. Across the ocean, even England's Queen Mother added them to her Christmas tree."

Collectors do not stop with a few of Radko's ornaments. They hang *hundreds* on their Christmas trees—900-plus in some cases, many found on eBay. Radko says his favorite is any ornament that brings a smile to someone's face.

"I love the stories they tell—some are as old as circa 1895. That's a lot of Christmases!," he says. "When I had my ornament company, some of my favorites were the fundraiser ornaments. In the course of twenty-five years, they raised over $3 million for breast cancer, AIDS, diabetes, heart disease, and pet charities." When Radko was designing ornaments, he favored a Vanderbilt gilded-age Victorian ornament that continues to sell well today. "I'm not much of a fan of pared-down Spartan design, which feels cold and computer-like," he says. "I prefer abundance, warmth, and enough visual stimulation to keep me mesmerized for hours, like a little kid in a huge toy store."

So how does the Czar of Christmas celebrate the occasion? "I love holidays because they remind us that there is more to life than just the daily grind," he says. "As we gather with friends, we make an extra effort to tidy up, make special foods, and bring on the music. These are all ways to celebrate life. So no style is right or wrong. Wherever I am, my celebration involves plenty of local holiday music and foods and the company of good friends."

When he is in Poland, he celebrates in the traditional Polish way, with candles on the tree, singing Polish Christmas carols, and enjoying an old-world Christmas Eve banquet with twelve kinds of fish and seafood. When he is in Hawaii at Christmastime, he surfs on Christmas morning. That night, he does the Mele Kalikimaka hula!

At home in New York State, Radko decorates the outdoors in November before it gets too cold. He spruces up the front door with a string of vintage red blinking bells set in pine boughs. Inside, he decks the halls, accompanied by a few friends and the sound of carols playing. He decorates two trees—both are typically white-flocked and pre-lighted, but he may use fresh trees one year and artificial trees the next.

Just in time for Christmas, a blanket of snow dusts Christopher Radko's stately house and grounds. Nutcracker toy soldiers guard the greenery-swagged entry and its twin star-topped trees. Inside, an ebullient Santa (played by the designer himself) welcomes visitors.
Photography courtesy Christopher Radko

"I love the look and scent of a natural tree. Noble firs are the most elegant," he says. "However, I like having my tree up for six weeks, so I may opt for well-made artificial trees. Each year they get better, more life-like." One year, his Christmas trees were on rotating stands and hung with double-sided lighted stars.

As for decorating style, "My trees are modern re-interpretations of trad-itional holiday décor—from the 1890s to the 1950s," he says. When I was growing up, my grandmother's tree was silver aluminum with all-blue orn-aments. I recall our neighbors outlined their front porch and trees with blue lights, too. It was a mid-century style that I enjoy bringing back."

Radko trims his living room in blue lights and mid-century blue and silver Shiny-Brites. "I add vintage 1950s mini-Italian lights. Hardwired with very slender wires, they retain their color for fine effect. It's amazing to me that older lights work much better than new ones. They were not meant to be disposable like mass-produced dec-orations today," he notes. "I take antique ornaments, such as Santas, stars, and reflectors, wash off the crackled old paint, and then repaint and re-glitter them. I use stained glass paints in blue, aqua, teal, and a touch of green. I accent the tree with Victorian paper die-cuts and chromolithographs, such as Santas and angels in blue. I carefully cut and then mount them, adding angel hair or spun glass and glitter."

He spends a lot of time in his cozy retro 1940s kitchen, so he puts a tree there, as well, with bright, late-1960s day-glo and candy-colored Shiny Brites. And there are a good number of plastic blow-mold ornaments that he has refurbished and re-glittered. "Let's face it," he laughs, "everything looks better with glitter!"

Many of Radko's Christmas decorations date from the late nineteenth and early twentieth centuries. An angelic Victorian-era child and greeting cards decorate a mirror. Holiday figurines, clusters of glass ornaments, and red taper candles adorn the mantel.

One of several trees is decked with brightly colored balls, shimmery garland, and a quaint pink-roofed church ornament. Santa and Mrs. Claus, Frosty, and a host of characters mingle amid wrapped gifts.

 Radko mixes different styles of ornaments with layers of beaded garlands and tinsel to create nostalgic trees with Victorian and retro appeal. The designer uses real tin tinsel to add shimmer.

Tree Trimming the *Radko* Way

Here is Radko's foolproof technique for decorating a Christmas tree.

"First, I wrap the trunk with tinsel garland (silver or gold, aqua blue, red, or a color that works for the tree).

"Next I string all the lights. I am careful to wind the strands up and down each branch to conceal the cords. I accent the tree with colored c-7 blinking mini-bulbs. (They add life to the tree.) I never use LEDs. I don't like their cold color, and it is wasteful to throw out perfectly good lights that I bought five years ago.

"When the lights are up, I place colored spheres inside the tree, near the trunk, for color and interest. Next, I add small ornaments on the top, using progressively larger ornaments as I work my way to the bottom. (It's important to check the spring cap of each ornament for sturdiness and re-stretch the wire spring if necessary.)

"Finally, I hang glass bead garland swags. And I use tinsel made of real tin from Germany that hangs straight down (unlike the cheap mylar version). Some of these items can be found through specialty dealers like Blumchen's and on eBay. The effect is gorgeous and just what I dreamed about when I was five years old."

Caring for Fresh Trees

- Choose a tree that is pruned with hand shears (not by a power shear that cuts the tree into a dense triangle like a shrub).

- Select a sturdy tree stand that is big enough for the trunk and will hold plenty of water.

- Make a fresh cut on the trunk before the sap re-seals. Be careful not to trim or shave off any bark (live capillaries are just under the bark).

- Water the tree with hot tap water (to keep the sap running smoothly) and keep water in the bowl of the tree stand.

- Add a few drops of bleach to the water to prevent mold growth. Add corn syrup, too—about one teaspoon daily to feed the tree.

COLLECTOR'S SOURCES

Golden Glow. "This amazing collector's club is dedicated to all things vintage and antique Christmas—anything more than forty years old," Radko says. "They hold a fun annual convention featuring educational exhibits and hundreds of antique Christmas item dealers. I love hanging out with over 600 others who love Christmas as much as I do." GoldenGlow.org.

The Christmas Museum of America. "This wondrous museum in Bethlehem, Pennsylvania, is open year round and exhibits decorations of yesteryear." www.NationalChristmasCenter.com.

At home with

Shayla Copas

Little Rock, Arkansas

An invitation to the home that Shayla Copas shares with her husband, Scott, and their King Charles spaniel, Roxie, is itself a Christmas gift. It's easy to see why Copas, owner of her eponymous residential and commercial interior design firm, has won so many holiday awards: *At Home In Arkansas* magazine named her one of Arkansas's 2015 Trendsetting Designers. In 2014, the Holiday & Decorative Association recognized her for "Best Christmas Tree in the Nation" for color and ornaments. That year it also named her the winner for Best Christmas Wreath Design in the US. Governor Asa Hutchinson appointed Shayla to the Arkansas Governor's Mansion Commission in 2015, and she designed the interior for Governor Hutchinson's inaugural ball.

Holidays are celebrated with "a multitude of soirees at our home with family and friends, while helping a worthy cause," says Copas, a board member of Easter Seals and an advisory board member for Children's Advocacy Centers of Arkansas. "Christmas is such a wonderful time to do this."

Guests are welcomed with the sight of glorious wreaths outside and inside, and Christmas trees star in the show. A self-described traditionalist, particularly at Christmastime, Copas usually decorates more than one tree and designs them around the colors in the room. "I have gone with a monochromatic color scheme in the past, but currently I am using more vibrant colors," she says. "Sometimes I choose a theme for the trees. When my daughter was young, I designed the most fabulous tree in her room with snowmen and snowflakes.

"We always go with an artificial tree," she adds, "and I use a different topper each year depending on my mood." However, many of the ornaments return each year, particularly her favored glass ornaments and gold cherub ornaments. "We decorate the foyer, formal living room, library, dining room, kitchen, and powder rooms," she says. "Next year I intend to decorate our master bedroom and the carriage house."

For the holidays, Copas loves glam—"anything that sparkles, and the more the better!"—such as the glittering, life-size rhinestone deer sculptures that recline on the grand piano in the entry foyer. Fireplaces also go glam. "I feel a mantel should be decorated elaborately. I hang a wreath above the mantel, and we hang stockings. Between us, Scott and I have four children and four grandchildren, so there are a lot of stockings to fill," she says.

Anticipating the family's arrival on Christmas Eve, "my husband and I start cooking the night before," Copas says. "After the meal, we like going to a movie as a family. My favorite thing about Christmas is family time. We are so fortunate to have each other."

The classic entry with sweeping stairs is elaborately decorated with boldly scaled garlands and wreaths. Handsome double doors swing open to welcome guests.

Opposite page Beyond the glittering rhinestone reindeer is a glimpse of the dramatic living room.

Roses on the coffee table are an early,
elegant symbol of Jesus.

Gold draperies in the living room are a
beautiful backdrop for the tree with its gold
and Tiffany-blue ornaments. The gold
cherub is one of Copas's favorite ornaments.

A garland, gold-trimmed wreath, and Tiffany-blue ornaments embellish the living room fireplace.

Previous page Festive red reigns
joyously in the Copas family room. Above
the mantel is a portrait of the Copas
family. *Photography by Janet Warlick*

Above In the family room, red and gold
decorations underscore the holiday spirit.

Shayla Copas's Tree Tips

Decorating strategy. I like to put my trees up first, then the garlands, then the ornaments .We start with the larger ornaments. When working on a budget, I use clusters to add drama. To create a cluster of small, solid-color balls, I put as many as five on a pipe cleaner. After the ornaments are on the tree, the topper is added, then the ribbon.

Color scheming. Don't be afraid to go tonal. A variation of one color can be quite dramatic.

Quality counts. Invest in quality décor. So many clients want to purchase from inexpensive sources. Those ornaments usually fall apart in a couple of years and then the client has to purchase ornaments all over again

Preserving artificial tree. I always dismantle the trees after the holidays. They will last longer that way. I have clients who like to store their trees fully assembled in the attic, but often the tree gets bent when it is shoved into the storage area. I have learned it is best to keep the original box for storage. Labeling the parts helps, too.

Caring for ornaments. I never leave ornaments on anything I design, except for wreaths. We store them on a wall in the garage and drape them with sheets. It is a good idea to store ornaments in heavy-duty, see-through plastic containers with labels. I keep similar ornaments in the same box and label them. I also store my ornaments according to room. For example, a label will say: library/ green glass finial. This makes putting ornaments up so much easier the next year. I wrap glass ornaments in paper.

"I feel a mantel should be decorated elaborately. I hang a wreath above the mantel, and we hang stockings. Between us, Scott and I have four children and four grandchildren, so there are a lot of stockings to fill."

At home with
Mary Helen McCoy

Memphis, Tennessee

Restrained seasonal décor keeps the focus on fine French antique furniture in the McCoy home. Above the mantel is a period oil painting of roses, McCoy's flower of choice for the season. A garland of greenery and chocolate velvet with gold-embossed bows drapes over the mantel, spilling onto the floor. Marble vases are filled with orange liex and greenery. A pair of French regence fauteuils, upholstered in a document fabric from Tassanari & Chatel, flank the fireplace. *Photography by Jay Adkins, courtesy Mary Helen McCoy Fine Antiques and Interiors*

Mary Helen McCoy loves the fragrances that signify Christmas. She also loves traditional Christmas carols. "I look forward to the sounds of Christmas," says the owner and CEO of Mary Helen McCoy Fine Antiques and Interior Design, Memphis. An antique dealer since 1987, McCoy is a member of dealer organizations worldwide, including the National Art and Antique Dealers Association of America (NAADAA), Art and Antique Dealers League of America (AADLA), *Confederation Internationale des Negociants en Oeuvres d'Art* (CINOA), and *Syndicat Nationale des Antiquaires* (SNA). In addition to supplying America's A-list interior designers with the finest antiques and art, she custom-designs pieces that are made in select ateliers in France.

When McCoy moved her business to Memphis in 2013, she and husband Ron (a director in the McCoy firm) moved into a historic house built in 1860 on the Buntyn Plantation and gave the house a fresh, sophisticated elegance.

Holiday decorating begins with hanging two artificial wreaths on the double front doors. "The first Christmas we were here, I discovered that hanging fresh greens on the doors was a bad idea," McCoy says. "The sun is too intense." Interiors are restrained and favor roses, the ancient symbol for Jesus (who was called the Rose of Sharon).

The dramatic foyer needs little holiday décor—only a pair of early twentieth-century French turned marble vases filled with creamy lisiathus. "The foyer is covered in a hand-blocked Clarence House wallpaper that is now discontinued," McCoy says. "The previous owner installed it thirty years ago. It has always been one of my favorite patterns and is glazed with gilded highlights."

She decorates with discipline, adding grace notes to the living room, dining room, powder room, and den. In the living room, a simple fresh garland on the mantel spills onto the floor and terminates with brown velvet and

A footed Lalique crystal bowl filled with roses graces antique nesting tables.

embossed gold bows. A pair of early-twentieth-century turned marble vases are filled with seasonal greenery and orange liex. "Keeping the mantel subtle is deliberate in a room filled with French antiques and decorative arts," she says. "This allows the other tabletop items and the Christmas tree to stand on their own." On the coffee table (an early-twentieth-century piece by Maison Jansen) is a French gilded and enameled crystal rose bowl (c. late nineteenth/early twentieth century). "I filled that with beautiful roses from my favorite flower shop, Garden District," she says. A porcelain jardinière on the Louis XV lady's writing desk contains seasonal greenery, berries, baby hydrangeas, and roses.

The eleven-foot fraser fir is the ideal height for the twelve-foot ceilings. "When buying a tree, take the stand to be certain that it will support the tree," she says. "We have a heavy-duty stand with a deep well for water."

McCoy decorates her tree with the 2004–2005 Angel Tree collection of ornaments from the Metropolitan Museum of Art, as well as the museum's French Renaissance gilt metal ornaments and enameled art nouveau ball collection in large and small sizes. These are paired with beautiful Waterford and other glass ornaments she found at TJ Maxx, and Radko ornaments. "My Christopher Radko ornaments consist of gold and silver glass stars along with a silver and gold-beaded glass garland from the same collection, which I bought in 1999," she says. "I have some wonderful red glass balls with gold from Radko, along with a selection of glass fruits that I adore. To complement the fruit ornaments, I purchased a series of nuts, pine cones, and acorns ornaments (in earthy colors as well as reds) from a Christmas shop in Charleston, South Carolina, where we were based for five years."

In McCoy's mind, no tree should be without birds. Hers are clip-on gold glass birds with feathered tails and gold-glittered birds whose feet attach to the branches with wire. A gilt metal Renaissance star from the Met takes pride of place on the treetop and is set off with gold bows and streamers.

The dining room table centerpiece—a candelabra and her mother's antique English Sheffield plate epergne with cut crystal bowls—is there year-round. She dresses it up with seasonal greenery mixed with roses and hydrangeas from Garden District, and adds pine cones sprayed with gold. On the buffet, an artificial garland of pine and pine cones is mixed with cut greenery (which was soaked for a couple of days) and red berries. A cut-crystal footed vase on the Louis XV carved walnut commode by Pierre Hache is filled with greens and white roses.

One Christmas ritual that Mary Helen observes is baking Greek pastries, using recipes that have been handed down for generations. "To friends and family we give a good bottle of wine and a tin filled with the Greek pastries," she says.

The eleven-foot fraser fir is decorated with ornaments from Christopher Radko and Waterford, and with French art nouveau balls. McCoy included antique cut-crystal prisms, fruits, acorns, and pine cones. Believing that no tree is complete without birds, she added gilded birds and peacocks. Golden bows and streamers set off the gilt Renaissance star topper from the Metropolitan Museum of Art.

A Jay Strongwater bejeweled cross ornament presages the coming Easter season.

On the Louis XV ladies writing desk, a nineteenth-century French porcelain jardinière holds berries and baby hydrangeas. Above the desk hangs a Regence mirror.

Sofa pillows made from a seventeenth-century tapestry are trimmed with antique metallic fringe. Decoupage boxes displayed atop the coffee table were made by McCoy's mother in the 1960s. The amber crystal and bronze lamps and bronze and marble end tables were custom made.

Roses fill a gilded and enameled crystal bowl on the coffee table.

In the dining room, roses highlight the coffee and tea service. On the dining table, McCoy mixes roses and hydrangeas with gilded pine cones and greenery from her favorite source—the Garden District shop—to fill the antique English Sheffield epergne. Red berries and a mix of pine and artificial greenery grace the seventeenth-century French Renaissance buffet. On the wall are nineteenth-century French Palissy ware platters with crabs *en relief.* At the Fortuny-draped bay window, a pair of tulip-filled late nineteenth-century French Barbotine vases sit on the eighteenth-century walnut and marble table *à gibier.*

The Louis XV French walnut commode
holds an elegant silver service and
French faience charger. A pair of
nineteenth-century Palissy ware plaques
depicting fishes and shells flank the
Louis XV mirror.

The entry hall in the McCoy's historic house is a study in classic elegance, with greenery and white lisianthus atop an eighteenth-century French console, along with an eighteenth-century Chinese export platter.

Above Greenery, pine cones, and white roses cascade from a red tole and bronze jardinière dating from the French empire period. A quartet of antique classical Piranesi prints, framed in sleek black, hang above the mid-century modern black lacquer cabinet.

At home with
Cecil Hayes

Coconut Creek, Florida

Cecil Hayes is that *rara avis* who is a native Floridian. Since the 1970s, she has owned Cecil's Designers Unlimited, in Broward County, Florida. Named to *Architectural Digest*'s Top 100 list of influential designers in the world, she is the only designer from the South in that rare company, and was the list's first African-American. So she was perhaps the natural choice to design interiors for the African-American Research Library and the Cultural Center of Broward County. Hayes's work has been featured in the Cooper Hewitt Smithsonian Design Museum. She has also been inducted into The History Makers, the nation's largest African-American video-oral history collection, housed at the Library of Congress. A motivational speaker, she shares her experience and expertise with young people.

She is also the author of *9 Steps to Beautiful Living* and *The Art of Decorative Details*. Among her clients are movie stars Samuel L. Jackson and Wesley Snipes, music producer Tim "Timbaland" Mosley, and NBA and NFL athletes.

Hayes's front-door wreath is typically evergreen and adorned with silk flowers. She decorates the foyer, living room, dining room, and family room with objects collected through the years, and often transforms storebought items. To make a coffee table centerpiece, for example, she crushed last year's red and silver ball ornaments, using them as a base for vials of flowers. The "leaves" in the vases were soft, folded placemats.

The dining table centerpiece grew out of a visit to Pier 1 Imports, where she saw "these crazy, funny reindeer. They needed a sleigh, so I used a child's toy sled and made side rails out of a picture frame. Pier 1 has some unusual Christmas decorations—things other stores do not have."

Hayes has a special glass tree that requires no decoration, but the Christmas tree is always real. Ten to twelve feet tall and selected by the family, including the grandchildren, it is decorated in a transitional style. "We decorate the tree together while listening to Christmas music," she says. "Rather than having a theme, I focus on traditional Christmas colors—red and green with gold and silver accents. The ornament style changes from year-to-year, but the colors do not. I like large, natural ornaments such as pine cones and my eight-inch mercury balls."

Butterflies are a recurring motif. "I saw those colorful butterflies and bought fifty. Then I bought fifty more!" she says. All 100 butterflies, attached with thin wire, carry the ornaments up and around the spruce tree. Atop the tree is a repurposed butterfly metal sculpture, originally a table accessory. Hayes removed the wood base and her husband welded the pieces into a tree topper. Once in place, she says, it looked as though the smaller butterflies were flying up to meet the larger ones.

"I enjoy the decorating because, as an interior designer, it is the only time I get to be 'tacky,'" she says. But try as one might, it is difficult to spot anything tacky here.

One hundred butterflies, attached with thin wire, adorn the ten-foot spruce tree.

Florida interior designer Cecil Hayes decorates the family Christmas tree. *Photography by Darryl Nobles, courtesy Cecil's Designers Unlimited*

Following Page
Granddaughter Mikala Powell helps Hayes with the decorating.

Grandson Mikal Powell and husband Arzell Powell trim the tree.

The coffee table centerpiece touts traditional Christmas colors. Fantasy flowers with a tropical look are embraced by leaves— green placemats artfully folded by Hayes.

Following pages The dining table centerpiece is a reindeer sculpture purchased from Pier 1 Imports. The Hayes-created sleigh is a child's toy fitted with picture-frame sideboards and filled with beautifully wrapped gifts.

Above the living room console, a graceful swag of bronze netting embellished with *faux* fruits and berries adds drama to the bronze metal-paneled wall.

Opposite page The foyer plays up a Christmas in Florida theme using colors of the water and sky with accents of peach, pink, and white. Gold and silver tree branches in tall white urns are hung with shells, peacocks, frogs on surf boards, and glamorous ornaments.

Pine cones and red bromeliads in a wooden African bowl (originally intended for mixing flour for bread) lend a Mother Nature theme in the family room.

At home with
Rhonda E. Peterson

Atlanta, Georgia

"Ah, Christmas—my favorite holiday!" says Rhonda Peterson, owner of Rhonda Peterson Associates in Atlanta. Still looking very much like the model she was when represented by Elite Model Management, Peterson's practice focuses primarily on residential planning and interior design. She also writes a popular blog, "Rhonda E. Peterson, Stylish Spaces Designed for Living."

Christmas season begins Thanksgiving evening in the Peterson household. "From this point on, we decorate pretty much daily," she says. "The kids [Noah and Gillian] are still in school and want to be part of the decorating, so I accommodate them as much as possible."

As a child, her family had artificial trees with a color theme. "We even had a white-flocked tree," she says. "A light set on the floor bathed it in alternating colors of blue, red, and green. Each year the ornament colors would change. Gold ornaments on a green artificial tree were my favorite." Now, she says, "If we've decided not to buy an evergreen tree, we grab the artificial one from the garage and fluff the branches, molding them just so." The family kicks off the season by watching *Polar Express* and drinking hot chocolate—even if it's eighty degrees outside.

Rhonda's decorating style is a sophisticated, highly edited look that she nevertheless describes as eclectic. "I have favorite ornaments that go on the tree every year," she says. "Most are gifts from friends and reflect how well they know me. A Jonathan Adler silver elephant and a silver tortoise, given to me by different friends, really speak to where I was in my life at that particular time. I had enrolled in an interior design program and had been sleeping very little because of the course load. Did you know that elephants sleep two or three hours each day? For two years I was going through my elephant phase!

Rhonda Peterson opens her welcoming Christmas-green door. *Photography by Kimberly Murray, courtesy Rhonda Peterson and Associates*

In the entry foyer is a graceful iron and glass table purchased for the Peterson's first home. The black-and-white framed images are Hermès catalog pages.

Tiny trees with burlap-wrapped balls and pine cones and a sprinkling of faux snow evoke a holiday spirit.

Opposite page Fresh greenery stars in this ribbonless wreath.

And the tortoise—well, this is an easy one: It doesn't matter how slow you go, as long as you go!"

The tree topper is different every year. "The kids always making something to put there," she says. "There is something about this time of year that brings out their creativity. Noah and Gillian have trees in their bedrooms that they decorate with ornaments they've had since they were babies and those they've collected over the years."

Artificial wreaths on the kids' bedroom doors are decorated with "anything and everything, including McDonald's Happy Meals toys and party favors," Peterson says. "We use garlands, wreaths, and ribbons to decorate every windowsill downstairs and every flat surface. I like to use a lot of silver, mercury glass, and clear glass, along with candles. I light each one every evening because I love the glow." Outdoor entryway decorations typically include a wreath and small urns or trees flanking the door.

"We love driving through neighborhoods where residents have gone all out with their exterior décor," she says. "My hat goes off to them—it is a lot of hard work! When we're driving in the car we listen to a Motown Christmas CD, along with a great one from Pottery Barn that was given to me." Another treasured ritual is the evening movie time that stretches from Thanksgiving to Christmas day. "We watch all the classics: *It's a Wonderful Life*, *White Christmas*, *Miracle on 34th Street*, *A Christmas Carol*, and so many more.

"I try to have the decorations put away before New Year's Eve," Peterson adds, "so that my home is ready to accept all of the amazing things the New Year has to bring."

Previous pages Pottery Barn cubes echo the tree's Tiffany-blue and chartreuse ornaments. Paintings above the Bassett sofa are *Ire* (left) and *Kinship* by Steve McKenzie, Atlanta. The smoke-colored side table was a display prop at the Louis Vuitton shop where Peterson was a sales manager.

Left to right
A mirrored tray and ornament-filled glass bowl accent the cube footstool.

In the foyer, the smart green table was what Peterson calls "a steal" from Marshall's (many designers' secret source). She painted it a statement-making chartreuse. The white owl vase is one of many owl-motif items that Peterson began collecting after seeing what she recalls as a "three-foot owl high up in a backyard tree at my childhood home."

Grange bistro side chairs flank the breakfast table—a $50 flea market find!

In the dining room, silver inherited from her grandmother, sapphire and silver-beaded plates, silver bell napkin rings, and a silver camel teapot add a luxe look.

Red curtains and a fire burning in the family room fireplace create a cozy Christmas setting. On the mantel are large pine cones from the designer's parents' yard in Arkansas. While visiting in late fall or early winter, Peterson's family gathers colorful leaves, acorns, and pine cones that will be used on holiday wreaths and tables in her Atlanta home.

Favorite ornaments on the family room tree include a ballerina and her toe shoes from Saks Fifth Avenue and a host of other interesting ornaments by Peterson's children, Noah and Gillian.

A side table holds an artful arrangement of pine cones, acorns, and seasonal touches.

Peterson, Noah, and Gillian "take five"—a moment for family fun.

The serene master bedroom has just a
touch of Christmas—a white scented
candle in an elegant glass container on
a mirrored nightstand from Bombay
Company.

At home with
Stephanie Tuliglowski

Joliet, Illinois

Like so many interior designers, Stephanie Tuliglowski is multi-talented. In addition to being a licensed cosmetologist, she had a career in commercial art, working in advertising while also painting portraits of children and family pets. Later she turned to painting decorative faux finishes for interior surfaces and furniture and working with established interior designers. Her interior design work has been featured in local newspapers and *Enlightenment*, a lighting industry publication.

At her French country-style home in Joliet, Illinois, she hosts three annual decorating events for clients and friends. They are invited to browse unique European-style fabrics, furniture, art, and accessories, "finds" discovered on her shopping forays.

"Christmas is a time to enjoy making our home a cozy place to gather with family and friends over good food and conversation," she says. One ritual that she and her husband, Ray, share is wrapping presents for their children, Breyton, Ryan, Nicholas, and Sophia, who are now young adults. "About a week before Christmas, Ray and I meet in our bedroom and bring out the wrapping paper (purchased specifically for each child), boxes, and gifts. I set each gift inside a tissue-lined box and hand it to Ray, the wrapping king. He wraps each gift beautifully."

Tuliglowski says an artificial tree suits her family's lifestyle. "We traditionally have two trees. One is decorated with the children's colorful hand-made ornaments from their younger years. The kids like to hang their ornaments on *their* tree. It also has glass figurines (Santas and snowmen) and Polish, Czech, German, French, Swedish, and Italian pieces.

The second tree is European style and mostly red, with floral bouquets, fleur de lis balls, crystal drops, large reindeer, and a leopard-patterned skirt. With a glass of wine and holiday music queued up, the decorating begins.

"The trees have a sense of history—they are storybooks of our family's life," Tuliglowski says.

Stockings are hung on the stair with great care. "Ray and I try to be creative and thoughtful in selections for each child. It gives us great joy to see them get excited as they pull out each item," she says. On Christmas morning there are pancakes, sausage, bacon, and fruit before the fun begins. Other holiday fare includes honey baked ham, cheesy potatoes, broccoli salad, cold shrimp, and hearty soups. But, the *piece de resistance* is youngest son Nicholas's specialty—cheesecake.

When the festivities are over, Tuliglowski has a brilliant storage solution: a walk-in closet. "We leave the smaller tree intact," she says. "Ornaments are carefully wrapped in tissue and returned to their boxes. Old French baskets hold mercury candles and garland. Wooden flower bulb boxes hold stockings." And with that, the closet door closes on Christmas.

An evergreen wreath adorns the French armoire in the dining room at interior decorator Stephanie Tuliglowski's home. *Photography by Caitlyne Elizabeth White, courtesy Stephanie Tuliglowski Interiors*

"Our Christmas trees are storybooks of our family life," says the designer. The European-style tree in her French country living room features floral bouquets, fleur de lis balls, and crystal drops, along with large ornaments and a red leopard-print tree skirt. A family pet admires one of several trees. A tapestry adds rich color.

A trio of glass-domed winter scenes
decorates the bureau.

A rustic nativity scene is displayed on an
antique pine cupboard.

The dining table is set for a
holiday buffet.

Pottery stars on an iron demilune table.

Provincial pottery stars on the diningroom mantel, paper white bulbs in a handsome planter and a bouquet of fresh flowers mingle with berries and greens.

A fauteuil ornament calls to mind Tuliglowski's popular blog, *Sit On This*, about chairs she discovers, recovers, and updates for resale—like the red velvet chair that fairly sings noel.

The "children's tree" (a tradition begun when her children were young) sports Santa and snowman figurines. Handmade decorations are joined by Czech, German, French, Italian, Polish, and Swedish ornaments. Tuliglowski's three grown-up sons trim the tree. Left to right: Breyton, Ryan, and Nicholas.

Tuliglowski's favorite ornaments include a Valentine's-gift teddy bear, Eiffel Tower, and Arc de Triomphe.

At home with
Denise McGaha

Dallas, Texas

Denise McGaha's clients expect her to deliver a turn-key, concierge-level interior in ninety days or less. No problem—her roster of professional sports figures and uber-busy executives get luxury-look designs on time—every time! McGaha has also been brand ambassador for Currey & Company, a company known for its unique lighting, accessories, and home furnishings.

Dallas-based McGaha honed her eye at luxury retailer Neiman Marcus, helping launch NeimanMarcus.com. But she is no stranger to donating her talents to society's less fortunate. One of her favorite charities is Dwell With Dignity, which helps the formerly homeless furnish their homes. Its annual Thrift Studio fundraiser is a thirty-day pop-up shop in which top-notch designers such as McGaha create room settings using donated items from the Dwell With Dignity ware-

house, with sales proceeds supporting the program.

Christmas at the McGaha home is a family affair. There is one Christmas tree. When son Jaxon and daughter Jori were younger, they would have their picture taken with Santa at Neiman Marcus and then select an ornament from the store. "Thirteen years later, these are still our favorites," she says. "Our tree changes every year based on what is inspiring me, but it is always full of sparkle and memories. There is always an angel on top."

McGaha decorates the entry and living and dining rooms, and places fresh flowers in all the bathrooms. "I always use fresh greens," she says. "I change out fruits and fresh flowers each week. It makes everything smell like Christmas. And everyone in the family has a Christmas stocking—including our pets."

Trailing greenery and a pine-cone-laden wreath decorate the entry of the McGahas' Dallas home. *Photography by Dan Piassick, courtesy Denise McGaha Ineriors*

The mantel is festooned with generously
sized pine cones, pomegranates, and berries.
A golden horn decorates the shelves.

The McGahas' Christmas tree is laden with ornaments and pine cones. A simple wreath, tied with a bow, hangs over a mirror. Whimsical ornaments of toy soldiers and fantasy fish mingle amid glass balls.

Opposite page Cocktails at Christmas time often mean fine wines and spirits served from silver goblets. A silver bowl holds white and gold ornaments.

Touches of red in berries and centerpiece flowers add holiday color. McGaha sets her
holiday table with gold-banded glassware and decorative plates.

The breakfast room's bowl of ornaments and sprigs of greenery make for an easy centerpiece.

To dress the bedroom for the season,
McGaha hangs wreaths over the mirrors
and places bouquets of greenery and
ornaments on skirted tables.

A simple tree with fairy lights next to the bed is a perfect place for presents from Santa. The purple ribbon on a monogrammed wreath picks up hues in the botanical print pillows.

Previous pages A sleigh bed seems perfectly suited for the season. The beribboned wreath and greenery add holiday touches.

At home with
Lance Jackson
and
David Ecton

Atlanta, Georgia

Lance Jackson and David Ecton are founding partners of Parker Kennedy Living, an interior design firm and regency-style vintage furniture dealer in Atlanta. Jackson describes the firm's style as "preppy on the edge," achieved with lacquered furniture and a mix of textures, vintage details, and young colors and patterns. "Our interiors have Palm Beach overtones," he says.

For an *Atlanta Homes & Lifestyles* Home for the Holidays show house, for example, they "married classic blue and white with rattan, wood, and greenery, and added magnolias and bright red bows. The company's creative director, Jackson graduated from the Savannah College of Art and Design and developed several successful interior design divisions with international firms. Now his work, which includes product design, is largely in Alabama, Florida, Georgia, New York, North Carolina, South Carolina, Tennessee, and Texas.

Ecton studied in Venice, Italy, where he was involved in the excavation of an Etruscan ruin. "It was there that I learned the importance of how one's space affects the way one lives," he says. His circuitous route to interior design began at the University of South Alabama, where he studied international trade. After graduation, Ecton headed to Mexico City to work for the US State Department, and later earned an MBA in international trade. Working as a graphic artist during graduate school offered Ecton a creative outlet from crunching numbers. His first job was marketing director for an IT firm. "Staying abreast of technology is similar to staying up with the trends in design—one minute you are current, the next, dated," he says. A desire to do exporting and importing and design led him to found Parker Kennedy with Jackon.

As busy as they are, the two take time out to celebrate Christmas by hosting several dinner parties during December. The couple hangs a wreath of fresh magnolia leaves on the front door and wreaths inside the windows and throughout the house. "We decorate the foyer, living room, dining room, den, and upstairs hallways," Jackson says. "We are constantly bringing new treasures into the mix and changing things up. Rarely does anything stay in one place for long."

They also deck out two trees—one in the den, hung with handmade family ornaments, and a flocked artificial tree in the front living room. "It is full of vintage glass ornaments in pink, turquoise, silvers, greens, and so on," Jackson says. "We stick with the same theme every year—tradition with a twist."

The Christmas tree stars in the living room of designers Lance Jackson and David Ecton. *Photography by Christina Wedge, Christina Wedge Photograhy / Atlanta, courtesy Parker Kennedy Living*

Following pages Furnishings from a variety of periods joyfully coexist. English wing chairs are updated with a vibrant, large-scale print. The Louis XIV armchair faces a glass and gold metal coffee table and fierce Foo dogs.

Opposite page On the lacquered orange sofa/library table, Foo-dog lamps with pagoda-shaped shades flank an updated version of the German feather tree in a Chinese cachepot. A reclining deer base supports the tree. Beneath the table (with Chinese Chippendale sides) are twin bamboo stools in a bright chartreuse lacquer finish with leopard skin patterned covers.

Red-and-white gingham curtains create an exciting backdrop in the eclectically furnished dining area. The focal point—a mirrored Parson's table and gilt bamboo mirror with a pagoda-shaped crest—is accented with matching white bamboo lamps. Below the table are two blue-and-white porcelain garden stools. Flanking the mirror are decorative brackets with bright orange vases.

The table's bright green lacquered top is a foil for other colors in the room. Bamboo chairs with cane backs are lacquered snow-white and given coordinating green covers. The centerpiece—a brass bowl full of gaily colored Christmas ornaments—is a simple, elegant Christmas centerpiece. A wreath at the window and white amaryllis are finishing touches.

Below Menus with flowing script on blue paper are a colorful accent to place settings and sure to whet appetites.

Chinese blue-and-white containers are
filled with colorful Christmas ornaments.

The professionally flocked Christmas tree looks as though it's wearing new-fallen snow.

The Christmas tree is crowned with a pristine white glass ornament with a gold filigree pattern.

At home with

DesAnn Collins

Elyria, Ohio

DesAnn Collins's career began as a child, when she transformed a large McDonald's french fries carton—red on the outside, yellow-and-white-striped inside—into a wing chair for her Barbie doll. Yet she followed a curving career path that included retail and bank management before opening Design By DesAnn in 2006. At age forty-four, she was expected to take over her family's deli/bakery/catering business. However, she decided it was time to pursue her gift for design. Home staging seemed like a good way to start a business, so Collins received Ohio certification to teach staging to realtors. Since then, she has not looked back. In addition to private commissions, she does pro bono work for Home Depot Foundation's Homes for Veterans, as well as Enchanted Makeovers, a charity for homeless women and children.

Collins's volunteer work ramps up in early November, when she decorates the Bay Village Ohio Homes for the Holidays event, in addition to decking out clients' houses. "Christmas is my favorite holiday—I get to go over the top," she says.

Christmas at home with husband Tom Horseman and their son, Collin, means hosting the traditional Christmas Eve family gathering. Before Christmas Eve, family members gather to bake Hungarian kiflik (nut-filled crescent rolls). "We've done this for over twenty-five years," she says. "I'm delighted that my parents continue to enjoy this. To witness my tough, Vietnam-War-veteran cousin show his softer side by carefully rolling out each dough ball in memory of our grandma is pure joy."

Collins and her family trim five Christmas trees. Large fresh trees go in the living room and Collin's room. The dining room, master bedroom, and guest room get three smaller trees, some of which are artificial. "Tom and I usually go together to buy the trees now that Collin is older," she says. "We enjoy the time together and looking at Christmas light displays as we drive through the neighborhoods."

Tree trimmings tend to be opulent. "Our main tree has evolved over twenty-seven years," Collins says. "At the core of the decorations are strands of crystal beads— leftovers from my wedding gown. We didn't have much money our first year of marriage, so I created the strands and loops of beads myself. There is always a star at the top. And I mix natural elements with pink, gold, and green bulbs and angel

Lighted swags of greenery and large ornaments hanging from bare branches welcome visitors to the home of designer DesAnn Collins. Nestled in a forested area and with a blanket of snow, her house has all the charm of a Currier and Ives engraving. *Photography by DesAnn Collins, courtesy Design By DesAnn*

On the eighteenth-century English-style
buffet is a mini Christmas tree trimmed
with spiraling gold ribbon. Above the
buffet is Collins's wedding portrait.

In true Victorian more-is-more app-roach, Collins's Christmas tree (one of five) holds a dazzling assortment of ornaments. Strands of beads are her favorite ornaments.

ornaments—especially the angel ornaments that Tom's beloved Aunt Margaret made for us from my husband's mother's wedding gown. I'm very sentimental. Collin's tree is filled with multi-colored lights and traditional ornaments—all the ornaments he has ever made or been given."

The guest bedroom tree is a salute to John Wayne and a nod to her love of cowboys. "I have great childhood memories of watching John Wayne movies with my grandma," Collins says. "This tree has red bandanas and large wooden stars."

Every room in the house is decorated, and she even hangs a few large wreaths on trees on the lawn "so that we can see them when looking out the windows." Indoors, wreaths are hung on the second floor landing and on each bedroom door. "I create my own wreaths using items purchased at consignment and antique shops and flea markets," she says. "This way, I can add to or change out the wreaths yearly."

She also suspends a wreath from fishing line over the fireplace mantel so that it appears to float in front of the old round mirror. "On the mantel, I mix natural rustic elements with elegant items," Collins says. "I always have an abundance of white lights mixed with heavy evergreen garlands and big pine cones. I add white candles. All those little white lights and the candles reflecting in the mirror create a ton of sparkle. We tuck in a beautiful, white, simple, sleek angel figurine given to me by a dear friend. And I decorate the chandelier with sparkling faux ice, pearls, silver and gold."

Her favorite aspect of the Christmas holidays is the simple joy of giving to others. "To see the delight and twinkle in little children's eyes—it sounds simple, but I wish people could live with that spirit all year long," she says.

Chunky white candles in silver holders and pine cones painted white and sprinkled with glitter contrast richly with evergreen rope on the fireplace mantel.

Originally the living room, the formal dining room is large enough to entertain family and friends.

Tiffany-blue napkins repeat the color of chair seats. The centerpiece is a glass bowl holding a chunky white candle and surrounded with greenery, ribbon, and Victorian furbelows.

A low chest beneath the window is decorated with a carved wooden cathedral candlestick and a glorious assortment of greenery, glassware, and bric-a-brac.

A "tootsie-roll" pillow in Tiffany-blue is lavishly trimmed and beaded.

On the eighteenth-century English-style buffet is a mini Christmas tree trimmed with spiraling gold ribbon. Above the buffet is Collins's wedding portrait.

Charming vignettes abound. A nativity scene and Father Christmas tableau make their holiday appearance.

An austere Ansel Adams photograph contrasts smartly with the Victorian Christmas swag.

Collins fearlessly mixes metals—gold, silver, and others—and materials such as silks, satins, velvets, and moirés to stunning effect.

Gold ribbon embellishes the evergreen rope on the stair railing.

Opposite page
On the second-floor landing, a red plaid ribbon and pillow say Christmas loud and clear!

Clockwise

A flower-trimmed cowboy hat reveals Collins's love of cowboy lore.

The second-floor stair railing gets a full complement of evergreen rope and ribbon. Below is a group of Christmas-pink poinsettias.

For years, the Santa bells on the newel post were used to awaken Collins on Christmas morning.

The powder room contains a black-and-white photograph of grazing cows by Collins, winner of many photography awards.

A contemporary version of an antique German feather tree decorates the bedroom. The bed is enlivened with Christmas-red linens. Poinsettias add a holiday note to the dresser.

A view of the living room with the giant Christmas tree and light-trimmed windows shows off the infamous "leg lamp"—a recent tongue-in-cheek tradition.

At home with
Tina Lewis

Surprise, Arizona

Tina Lewis, owner of Happy Everything Lifestyle Designs, is happy wearing many hats—party planner, organizer, personal stylist, seasonal decorator, and, of course, interior designer. "I am so blessed to be able to incorporate all the things I love to do," she says. After teaching school for many years, Lewis earned a graduate degree in children's theater and creative dramatics. During summers, she taught English and American culture to girls from Toyko's Bunka University. People who knew Lewis loved to cook and organize began asking her to cater parties and weddings. Soon she left teaching and opened a catering business, which led to event planning and an etiquette consultant certificate from the Protocol School in Washington, DC.

Call it serendipity—her event planning clients liked her decorating style and began asking her to redecorate their homes, using many of their own items. (She also helped them perfect their own style of dressing.) "When I put my

home on the market, many realtors asked for the name of the person who staged it," Lewis says. "I began to include home staging in my services and received my certificate from Staging Diva. This led to my new business—Happy Everything Lifestyle Designs."

Lewis's forte is dramatic vignettes, and that means lots of Christmas trees. "My little cottage gets eight trees inside and outside," Lewis says. "They are all artificial; otherwise, I would be knee deep in pine needles." Each tree has a theme and is capped with an appropriate tree topper. Her favorite is a traditional French-themed tree decked out in red with touches of orange and tons of ornaments, including Eiffel towers. "At Christmastime, more is more!" she says.

The front door gets a wreath inside and outside; poinsettias are everywhere; and every room is decorated, including the bathrooms and laundry. Lacking a traditional mantel (after all, her cottage is in Arizona), Lewis sets a

copper wash tub, twinkle lights, greenery, poinsettias, and an angel on top of the gas fireplace.

Lewis hosts a breakfast following the Christmas Eve service. "Everyone opens one gift at a time while the others watch," she says. Throughout the entertaining season, "Every meal gets a different tablescape," she says. "And, of course, I design many other tablescapes during the season for parties with friends." A favorite event is hosting breakfast for a group of friends who shop together every Christmas.

"Breakfast with Santa" for girlfriends before a day of Christmas shopping is an outdoor affair. Santa plates and mugs on a vintage tablecloth set the tone for a meal featuring Easy Oven Omelet.
Photography by Ed Gower and Tina Lewis, courtesy Happy Everything Lifestyle Designs

121

Child-sized cowgirl boots—in Christmas red—add color and whimsy to a courtyard arrangement.

Opposite page The tabletop tree in the library features Christopher Radko Shiny Brite ornaments.

A tabletop tree gets an equestrian theme with horse ornaments and a jockey's cap.

A pillow with a special message and holly motifs adorns the red leather living room sofa.

Lewis treasures the stained glass nativity scene beneath the window in her cheerful kitchen—a gift from her mother. Other favorite things include her Christopher Radko Christmas tree cookie jar, a sugar plum cookie jar, French nutcrackers, and Santa boots and hats.

Lewis collects Santas from yard sales, thrift shops, and estate sales, and they are always the first thing she displays.

Past and present meet in a table setting featuring classic Spode Christmas tree dinner plates and contemporary reindeer dessert plates. The Christmas tree in an antique tub is trimmed with Christopher Radko Shiny Brite ornaments and fairy lights that make the room sparkle.

Caroler figurines atop an antique oak dresser greet visitors. Lewis created the snowscapes by filling lidded glass jars with cotton "snow" and tiny sculptures. The lamp is an antique coffee grinder.

Themed table settings are a Lewis specialty, like this vignette with a music theme The unexpected black-and-white table cloth is countered with old cranberry-red chargers and Aunt Isabelle's martini glasses.

A Madonna and child figurine is paired with ivy topiary.

It takes Blalock several days to trim her tree with ornaments she began collecting in her teens.

At home with

Gloria de Lourdes Blalock

Arlington, Virginia

While Cuban-born Gloria de Lourdes Blalock misses Noche Buena, the traditional Cuban Christmas Eve she grew up celebrating with her family in Deerfield Beach, Florida, she has developed cherished traditions with her own extended family.

Christmas Eve dinner and Christmas brunch bring the family together at her mother-in-law's home, where a beautiful table is set with family heirlooms including an antique lace tablecloth that belonged to her mother-in-law's mother, and china, crystal, and sterling handed down from her father-in-law's parents. "I always say that Christmas doesn't feel real until I enter their home on Christmas Eve," Blalock says. Back home by late afternoon, "I always take a nap," she says. "Falling asleep on Christmas day in the glow of the Christmas tree is a treat that I never take for granted."

The Blalocks have a main Christmas tree in the living room and a smaller tree in each bedroom. Her children,

Kailee and Cullen, decorate those in their bedrooms. The master bedroom tree is artificial, and she inserts some of the real tree's trimmings to add fragrance.

The living room's eight-foot fraser fir has over 1,200 lights, 800 ornaments, and yards and yards of ribbon to add texture. "When it comes to the main tree, I sometimes wish I could take off the decorator's hat and relax, but I can't!" she says. "There have been years when I wish I could just group three trees together and not place anything on them. But our 1904 arts and crafts bungalow just feels like home when it's decorated to the nines."

That includes white lights and evergreens draped from the porch piers and an abundance of wreaths, bows, red glass balls, and fresh juniper that stand out against the chocolate-colored bungalow.

Even experienced designers have the occasional disaster. "One year the tree fell forward because I didn't have enough

weight on the back," Blalock says. "Sadly, I lost some precious Christopher Radko ornaments and other glass ornaments that were just gorgeous. The next year I made sure the weight was evenly distributed."

Living just minutes from the nation's capitol, Blalock has many White House Christmas ornaments received as gifts or found at garage sales and on eBay. Her goal is to collect two each from as many years as possible so that she can pass on a full set to her children. Another favorite is the glass Cuban cigar ornament she received from Ana Casanueva-Perez, a fellow Cuban whom she first met on Facebook.

Blalock prefers a traditional red and gold color scheme. "When I lived in Miami, I used pale pink, sea-glass green, and clear glass balls of varying sizes," she says. "Ornaments were pastel sand castles, miniature wreaths, and painted carousel ponies." Now those ornaments go on the master bedroom tree. The main tree's topper is a mir-

Garlands and candles in glass containers add romance to the fireplace.

Twin ceramic garden stools flank the fireplace.

Opposite page
A star is just one of the more than 1,000 ornaments Blalock cherishes.

Following pages
Ornaments hang from bare branches backing white orchids on the mantel.
Photographs by Laura Jens Photography

rored star like the one that guided the Three Magi.

On the mantel, Blalock typically creates a tableau around her collection of golden pheasants from the 1930s to the 1960s, adding fresh and artificial greens and a nativity scene. Behind it hangs a painting by her brother, Rolando Mendez, named *My Sister's Happiness*. "When the lights are dim and I look toward the mantel during the Christmas season, my heart simply sings with happiness," she says.

And the holidays wouldn't be complete without the Christmas disco dinner on December 27. "My in-laws come over for a fancy pizza dinner served with the lights down and disco music playing in the background," she says. "We are known to get up during dinner and dance to our favorite songs. Once all ten of us formed a conga line and danced from the dining room to the living room.

In a nod to her roots, Blalock leaves the decorations up through January 6, known as the Day of the Three Kings. "This is what they celebrate in Cuba and in other Latin American countries and Spain," she says.

At home with

Gary E. Mullis

Hazelhurst, Georgia

Spells Mansion is one of the most talked-about houses in Jeff Davis County. Built in the mid-1870s by Glenn and Sara Beth Spell, it saw many owners but was never lived in until events designer Gary E. Mullis, owner of 341 Antiques & More in Baxley, Georgia, bought it in September 2011.

Neglected and vandalized, for many years, the house was a notorious eyesore. The wiring and plumbing had been stripped, and the grand elements such as marble walls, elaborate mantels, decorative flooring, chandeliers, and even cabinet doors had been removed. The interior walls were covered in graffiti, and most of the windows were broken. There was wood rot, mold, and mildew. The grounds were so overgrown that two side wings were not even noticeable from the entry. "A contractor told me that the only thing of value was the brick on the exterior walls," Mullis says.

But he saw graceful architecture and great bones. Mullis worked with his father, Edwin Mullis, and others to restore the house, and in Christmas 2014 hosted an open house to benefit special-needs children. Visitors were awed, beginning with the sight of twin eight-foot garland swags decorated with peacock feathers and greenery on the front doors. "The paired swags set the tone for what was to come," Mullis says. But no one could fully anticipate the world of Christmas that he created inside the new Spells Mansion.

A massive Bohemian crystal chandelier in the front foyer is from the Czech Republic. A large French chandelier hangs in the formal living room. In the dining room is a brass chandelier from Turkey. And the granddaddy of them all—a Baccarat hand-cut crystal chandelier found in central Florida—hangs in the rear foyer.

But it is the Christmas trees of Spells Mansion that visitors come to see. More than twenty-seven—all artificial—are on display against a backdrop of fine antique furniture. "Artificial trees do better in supporting a large number of ornaments," Mullis says. "And, they fare better on display over a long period of time." Trees range in height from three to fourteen feet. "One eighteen-foot tree remains in the attic, just waiting to be put up," Mullis says. "Hopefully, in the future this tree will be placed in the twenty-six-foot-high foyer."

Tree trimming starts the day after Thanksgiving and continues until December 24. "Purchasing the house made it possible for me to display my more than 20,000 ornaments for the first time," Mullis says. Trees in each room of the mansion are trimmed to complement the room's mood. Some trees have as few as fifty ornaments, some as many as 4,000.

The seven-and-a-half-foot foyer tree, which Mullis named "Chill of Winter," is decorated in cut glass or crystal and silver and stands on a revolving, glass-topped table with a carved wood swan base. Giant snowflakes are suspended from the second floor, and a six-foot-high bohemian crystal chandelier hangs above the tree.

Spells Mansion—once thought
haunted—was the scene of filming for
an episode of Edgar Allen Poe's Mystery
Theatre shown on GPTV on Halloween
night 2014. *Photograph by Gary E.
Mullis, courtesy of Spells Mansion*

Double doors (c. 1800) are decorated
with eight-foot-high swags. *Photograph
by Gary E. Mullis*

Doors open to a dazzling crystal and silver tree. *Photograph by Debra Tanner Gary E. Mullis*

Opposite page Antique doors establish a sense of elegance in the two-story entry hall. Up close, the crystal and silver tree captivates. *Photograps by Debra Tanner Gary E. Mullis*

All ornaments on the essentially silver tree are glass, preferably crystal.
Photograph by Gary E. Mullis

The fourteen-foot living room tree, laden with 3,500 ornaments, is one of twenty-seven Christmas trees in the house.
Photograph by Gary E. Mullis

The mantel in the formal living room is one of nine that replace missing original mantels. *Photograph by Debra Tanner*

Of all the decorative clocks in the house, the baroque Putti clock is Mullis's favorite. *Photograph by Gary E. Mullis*

The formal living room features a fourteen-foot tree in front of a floor-to-ceiling window dating from the 1800s. This tree has more than 3,500 ornaments. The 1878 baby grand piano holds a traditional LED-lit Christmas tree that captures almost every color of light, Mullis says. A large taxidermied bobcat watches from atop the piano. Between the formal living room and den, two gold metal, branch-like fixtures are hung with glass Santa ornaments and family-photo ornaments. The fireplace mantel is lit with LED candles and draped with pine and evergreen garland embellished with bronze and gold glass ornaments. A rococo mirror soars six feet above the mantel. A swag with bronze and gold ornaments hangs above the mirror.

An arched opening separates double parlors that are now a den and formal living room. *Photograph by Debra Tanner*

Over 400 nutcrackers decorate the den, also known as the Nutcracker Room. Santa's portrait above the mantel is surrounded by a giant, nutcracker-ornamented swag. Life-size nutcrackers stand guard in niches flanking the archway. *Photographs by Debra Tanner*

The den, known as the Nutcracker Room, contains more than 2,500 nutcracker ornaments by manufacturers such as Old World, Polonaise, and Steinbok, and more than 2,000 Radko Celebration ornaments. The mantel is heavily decorated with nutcrackers surrounding the large Santa oil painting. Glass heart-shaped ornaments dangling from the mantel represent fallen US soldiers. Six-foot nutcrackers stand guard in niches flanking the doorway. On the Louis XIV desk near the entry is a small tree decorated entirely in red. Several crystal nutcrackers are standing on the desktop and small LED lights allow the beautiful crystal prisms to refract all the colors of the rainbow.

Opposite page The dining room (Peacock Room) becomes the Radko Room at Christmastime. Its 4,000 Christopher Radko ornaments outshine the mounted peacock and peacock items that honor Mullis's grandmother and her pet peacock. *Photographs by Gary E. Mullis*

The mantel is trimmed with fragrant rosemary springs and ornaments. *Photograph by Gary E. Mullis*

The dining room, formally called the Peacock Room, was created in memory of Mullis's maternal grandmother, Allowee, and her pet peacock. During Christmas, it is considered the Radko Room and is decorated in traditional Victorian style. Six trees are hung with more than 4,000 Radko ornaments collected over the years.

On the dining table are two gold metal Radko trees with more than 200 Radko ornaments. In the center of the table, hanging from the brass chandelier, is yet another Radko display—a gold metal turntable, chandelier-like ornament holder with more than fifty Radko ornaments hanging from it. The elegant fireplace mantel in the dining room is adorned with fine artificial evergreen swags highlighted with eight ornate glass ornaments.

The large dining table is always set for twelve guests with Homer Laughlin china in Christmas colors that can be used year-round. (Mullis later discovered that Depression-era movie theaters had a "dish night," where they gave out dishes in this lovely French pattern to get people into the theaters.) The table is not set traditionally. He described his unique table setting as "simple, ready, now let's eat."

Radko ornaments adorn the table trees and chandelier. *Photograph by Gary E. Mullis*

The table is set in Mullis's idiosyncractic style. *Photograph by Gary E. Mullis*

A tall Santa figure greets visitors to the breakfast room. The largest of four trees sits in the center of the room. *Photograph by Gary E. Mullis*

The breakfast room has four trees. The largest in the center of the room sets atop a table with a bronze base featuring monkeys. Mullis says that the "tree" is made of iron and can hold up to seventy-five ornaments. On the buffet is a four-foot-tall "Radko tree" with miniature Santas.

Two wall-hung trees bring Christmas cheer to the kitchen. *Photographs by Gary E. Mullis*

Five trees enliven the kitchen.
Photographs by Debra Tanner

The kitchen has five trees, including two six-foot-tall trees that hang on the wall. "They are decorated with items that represent something from one of the four food groups, wines or other drinks, or something used for food preparation," Mullis says. On the kitchen island is another six-foot tree decorated with food and utensil ornaments (pie slices, cheeses, candy, tiny coffee pots, pans, forks, and spoons).

The laundry room tree is whimsically decorated with clothing-item ornaments such as shirts, shoes, and dresses.

On the rec room shelves—safely out of
easy reach—is Mullis's extensive collection
of "celebrity" dolls. *Photograph by Debra
Tanner*

The lower level. Beyond the den is a secret passage to the lower-level game room and guest quarters, originally built as a fallout shelter. At the bottom of the stair, around the wine closet are antique toy cars and Hallmark ornaments. Above the wine rack are superheroes from nearly everyone's childhood, including Superman, Batman, and Marvel Comics heroes. A stone lion fountain near the wine rack is surrounded by artificial greenery. Mullis added a fog machine to the water fountain, making the basement even more dramatic.

"On entering the game room, one's attention goes to the novelty tree," Mullis says. "It's decorated with more than 400 ornaments representing television superstars, pro-athletes, comic strip characters, and movie and television personalities. Guests stand at this tree for a long time reminiscing about their favorite TV, movie, or childhood heroes such as Elvis, Marilyn Monroe, *I Love Lucy*, and *Three Stooges*, he says. On open shelves are more than 100 vintage and antique dolls depicting famous people, including US presidents and actors. Flickering backlights against the large stained glass windows flanking the fireplace give the impression of changing light outdoors.

The tree in the *guest suite*— otherwise known as the Green Room— is decorated entirely with green ornaments. Standing near the fireplace are two rustic gold deer wearing Christmas lights. In the reading nook is a white-flocked tree with green and white glittered branches. The guest bathroom contains a gold metal tree with a variety of glass ornaments, including Polonaise, Old World, Radko, and others.

The master bedroom tree has a flora and fauna theme with red berries, wildlife animals, and the like. In the master bath, a seven-foot, all-white tree is decorated solely with blue glass balls that complement the Roman-style black marble tub.

"The *girls' room* is home to a large white tree decorated with animal ornaments, including a variety of canine breeds recognized by the American Kennel Club. Another smaller tree in the girls' bathroom is hung with "large ornaments made to look like diamonds and other precious stones—anything that shines," Mullis says.

The *boys' room's* nautical theme is reflected in the tree ornaments such as boats and sails, while the tree in their bath has a fishing theme.

The third-floor *media room* contains six white trees, each placed in a large window so that it can be seen from afar. They have white lights and no ornaments to detract from their winter beauty.

With so many ornaments, Mullins says it would be impossible to pick a favorite. However, the ornaments his sister makes each year are special, along the Radko ornaments honoring 9/11 and the twelve days of Christmas. As for tree toppers, most are made each year from an assortment of ornaments or items found at home or in the woods.

"On Christmas day, all family members are present and we start with the opening of stockings—the highlight of the celebration," Mullis says. "Then there is a feast, followed by a gift exchange. Being with family and friends, enjoying all the celebrations and décor, seeing the joy on each person's face as they fellowship with each another, and the expressions on the kids' faces as they open their gifts are what I enjoy most."

Spells Mansion was bought and sold so many times that it was never honored during the holidays. "Now it is a showplace, Mullis says. "Hundreds of visitors come through each year at Christmas to see this beautiful house as it was meant to look many years ago. As the seventeenth owner, and the only one to complete it and live here, it pleases me to call Spells Mansion home, especially at Christmastime."

Only green ornaments are allowed in the Green Room (guest suite). *Photograph by Debra Tanner*

 A few of Mullis's thousands of ornaments: Dorothy's red slippers; red, white, and blue heart-shaped American flag ornaments; a Scottish bagpiper; a historic house; and a Florida state ornament. *Photographs by Gary E. Mullis*

The entry gets Mullis's star treatment with overscaled ornaments and greenery. *Photograph by Gary E. Mullis*

At home with
Keith Carrington

West Palm Beach, Florida

Celebrating Christmas in a strictly trad-itional way is not exactly interior designer Keith Carrington's cup of tea. His penchant for bright color, eclectic items, and fanciful fun make his holiday a celebration of all that is glorious in the paradise of Palm Beach.

His quixotic mix of vintage lighting and ornaments and objects d'art makes his approach to seasonal decorating spectacularly idiosyncratic. The whim-sical "bigtop tent" foyer features an orange and white banded ceiling that transforms the space into a three-ring circus. Atop the foyer's bureau plat, a Buddha's head shares a tableau with an ornament-studded wreath, illuminated branches, and a pair of Christmas-tree-inspired objects. Nearby, a kimono is surrounded by poinsettias. A reindeer keeps company with seashells and a bowl filled with shiny ornaments on the center round table. Nostalgic Santas mingle with seashells and antique rose medallion plates in the hand-painted faux red malachite secretary.

Exuberantly layered, vibrant hues never seem to be too much for Carrington's reimagined 1940s-era house. "Every year it's different in color scheme and mood," says Carrington, who typically starts decorating on December 1. "This year's color scheme was orange, purple, and turquoise because my tree was in the foyer, and the colors worked with my Ralph Lauren women's couture fabric made into curtains."

Every room gets decorated to some degree—"even the bathroom gets at least a jingle bell or two." He prefers two trees, a main tree in the Florida room and another small tree in the kitchen. "The main tree's design changes with the mood du jour," he says. "But the kitchen tree (composed of pale turquoise feathers) always features antique chandelier crystals with the tiniest vintage hand-blown mini-ornaments."

Carrington notes that not everything has to be elaborate to be festive. "My kitchen tree motto is KISS (keep it

simple, stupid). It's a great motto to live by, as well, I might add." Sometimes just a simple change of ribbon color and feature ornaments does the trick of updating a look, he notes.

For the main tree, however, Carrington likes the "more is more" approach. His latest tree was inspired by 1950s and '60s style. After discovering a source for mid-century bubble lights, the designer went retro-chic, pairing the lights with vintage glass ornaments. "My tree has traditional elements since I mainly use vintage ornaments, but I always twist it up a bit," he says. He placed his tree in the center of the room on a table, but to gain access to power to light the tree, Keith had an electrician replace the hanging lantern with an outlet and

Opposite page Under the foyer's circus big top, a red-nose reindeer and vintage Santa Claus announce Christmas is here. *Photography by Nicholas Sargent, Sargent Photography, courtesy Keith Carrington Interiors*

A festooned chandelier lights the foyer. Tropical foliage and poinsettias add lively natural notes.

Carrington accessorizes a stately secretary with his collection of vintage Santas and knickknacks from childhood. The display includes decorative porcelain and a gilded seashell, lest one forget this is Florida.

Following pages Turquoise, orange, and saturated citrus hues replace traditional red and green in designer Carrington's Palm Beach home.

halogen down lights to graze the tree, bathing it in a tinted gel-wash of color.

Carrington's favorite ornaments are from childhood. One of the most cherished is a "small snowman bell that I used to ring first before anyone was allowed to open presents," he recalls, noting that "even in my youth I liked to orchestrate events." Another treasured ornament, a fragile, German hand-blown Santa with hints of the original poly-chromed surface, belonged to his great grandmother. He is also fond of a vintage Santa bubble light that was his night light when he visited his grandparents at Christmastime. Other favorite decorations include a pair of vintage hand-sewn felt stockings from childhood. "They are so cool that I'm thinking of having them re-created for sale," he says.

Carrington likes the scent of live trees, although they often need help to make them last well into the New

Year. He has his trees professionally flocked, a process that adds the look of snow and sometimes color and keeps pine needles in place for the season. He topped a recent tree with "a huge double-sided red bow with ribbon streamers cascading down the tree," a simple but dramatic finale.

Windows are decorated with lit garlands wrapped with big shiny balls. A self-proclaimed "wreath-aholic," Carrington decks the front gates and main door with wreaths. "Since I'm living in Florida, a real wreath outside would get fried in the sun in one day, so I resort to artificial wreaths, sometimes simply covered abundantly with ornamental balls," he says.

Carrington's festive holiday celebrations include a mix of friends, clients, and business associates on whom he bestows gifts such as the homemade jams he spent the summer "putting up." "Everyone loves gifts from the heart," he says.

Keith Carrington | 159

The eclectic mix of vintage ornaments, antique furnishings, and pop culture references reflect designer Carrington's skill at blending old and new. Curtains are made of Ralph Lauren fabric.

Every room receives a "jingle."
A bow, says the designer, is often enough to add a holiday note.

A capiz-shell pendant lamp hung with turquoise beads and vintage bubble lights shares space with a canopied day bed.

Previous pages Carrington places his main tree atop a round table in the Florida room. Swags of greenery, laden with vintage glass balls and fairy lights, surround the window. Stockings from his early childhood nestle in the garland. Stark white frosted branches with fairy lights flank the sofa.

Old window panes are painted with
nostalgic winter scenes for use as wall art.

At home with

Pam Kelley

Highland Park, Texas

Dallas-based Pam Kelley founded Pam Kelley & Associates in 1974. Her premier Park Cities firm is known for innovative design rooted in southern tradition. Kelley's residential and commercial projects take her coast to coast and across the pond. So as Christmas approaches, focusing on her own home is a welcome change of pace.

"Decorating my home has never been a family project. I am too detail-oriented to let anyone else help," she says. "The task of assembling and decorating two trees can be overwhelming, but I thoroughly enjoy every minute of it. The finished product is my gift to family and friends."

The tree in the formal living room can be admired from the dining room and the street, and the second tree is in the family room. She no longer uses real trees. "I love their authenticity and fragrance, but now I do beautifully crafted artificial trees, lightly flocked," Kelley says. "I prefer a lightly flocked tree to look as if it has just been dusted

with fresh snow. The flocking makes the ornaments stand out."

The trees are pre-lit and fire resistant—two bonuses—and there are no LED lights for Kelley. "My lights must be warm and on a dimmer; I adore a very soft glow," she says.

While her traditional style and color scheme remain constant year after year, the number of ornaments grows, thanks to her extensive travels. "I do not buy anything unless it is very special," she says. "For example, I have a terrific collection of gold and bronze-dipped leaves unique to the states and countries I have visited." Kelley also collects vintage glass ornaments and has blown glass ornaments from the early days of Christopher Radko. "Opening and unwrapping the baubles is like opening a thousand little presents each year," she says. A *thousand*? Yes, literally. "I unpack them and group them. That process alone takes a day. Every ornament has a story; each one reflects a memory."

Kelley's most treasured ornaments are antique German pieces from the F. W. Woolworth Five & Dime in Houston. "My father was store manager there when I was a little girl," she says. "I have only a few cherished pieces. I know this is where my love for the blown glass beauties started."

A German wax angel tops the tree. "Her face and hands are gently molded from wax by artisans in Europe," Kelley says. "I feel as if the tree is almost magical, and I love to sit alone and stare at its beauty. The tree is like a vista into a special wonderland.

Kelley dresses the family-room mantel in garland that she makes from bits and pieces of greenery. Eight velvet-backed needlepoint stockings—another Kelley creation— are hung from a simple mantel in the living room. Outside, wreaths in the protected entryways are covered in vintage glass ornaments.

Holiday traditions at the Kelley home begin with an early Christmas Eve mass. "Usually it's the children's mass," she

The decorated front porch, with monogrammed pillows bearing the address, greets holiday visitors.

Pam Kelley's home, historic 4656 Southern Avenue, is a neoclassical structure designed by James Duff and built in 1939. *Photography by Dan Piassick, courtesy Pam Kelley and Associates*

says. "Our family dinner is at my house, with my sons, daughters-in-law, and grandchildren. This is a small dinner and quite dressy. We indulge in ice-cold oysters-on-the-half-shell to start. This part is so much fun. We stand around the kitchen island and drink champagne and eat the oysters while the kids play and beg to open presents. Next, we have beef tenderloin, mashed potatoes, and a salad. After dinner is finished, we gather around one of the trees and open the presents. Christmas Eve can be a very late night."

A second celebration takes place around 4:00 p.m. at Kelleys' home. "We have a festive Mexican dinner of tamales, rice, and beans. Then we host a lively and loud gift exchange for the children," she says. "We end the evening enjoying sweets, including Mexican wedding cookies and traditional sugar cookies." Christmas decorations stay in place until after Epiphany on January 6.

Graceful greenery and branches of red holly berries in blue and white
Chinese export vases add seasonal drama to the living room mantel. Kelley made the
eight needlepoint stockings awaiting Santa's visit.

The ceiling-height living room tree looks like something from a Victorian-era postcard.

The family gathers around the marble fireplace on Christmas afternoon.

The family room tree is laden with vintage ornaments and old-fashioned tinsel.

Each wrapped gift receives Kelley's custom treatment.

Above Hand-dipped gold leaves (collected on worldwide travels) become shimmering tree ornaments. An aspen leaf and a Canadian maple leaf are shown.

Vintage postcards take center stage among the branches.

The beaded peace ornament is one of Kelley's favorites.

This nature-inspired vignette includes a vintage postcard from Kelley's collection.

A nearly translucent glass egg is one of the many hand-blown ornaments.

An eighteenth-century English secretary
holds bits of Christmas past, including
the hand-carved cross and madonna, both
cherished gifts.

The Georgian dining table awaits Christmas Eve dinner. Copper chargers enhance the antique English china and French cutlery. Silver napkin rings are engraved with the names of family members.

On the eighteenth-century sideboard, a blue-and-white porcelain lamp casts a soft glow on a madonna and child figurine.

Opposite page A silver English samovar and fresh fruit add seasonal elegance in the kitchen.

The carriage house/design studio's décor
complements the main house. Soft
twinkle lights on a magnolia tree and
decorated table tops add festive notes to
the garden.

At home with
Jamie Gibbs

Indianapolis, Indiana

The holiday season starts early for Jamie Gibbs and his partner, Paco Argiz. They entertain in their spacious Indianapolis home, which they renovated extensively on the heels of one of Gibbs's ambitious projects, directing the restoration and green renovation of Dulcinea, the historic Indianapolis mansion.

The couple is at home with a crowd. "We host our famous Paco's Tacos party on Saturday after Thanksgiving (the menu starts with leftovers from Turkey Day). This year we had sixty-six people at the taco party," Gibbs says. Christmas preparations begin the following Sunday.

"With the help of our house man and maids, it takes Paco and me about a week—or until I am exhausted—to be ready for Christmas," Gibbs says. A busy product design consultant and designer of six signature collections (including the Vintage Collection for D'Kei Inc.), he doesn't alter his pace, just his focus. He serves on several boards, including the Indianapolis Opera Company, the Horticultural Society of

the Indianapolis Museum of Art, the Fund for Park Avenue, and CIVITAS. Prior to forming the New York-based international interior design and landscape architecture firm Jamie Gibbs Associates, he was Indiana's director of design in the division of state parks.

"We really enjoy the *people* aspect of the holiday—seeing our family and friends, watching their faces light up as they recognize ornaments, telling

Christmas lights on topiaries in Haddonstone planters, swags and wreaths on the balcony, and decorations at the doorway to Jamie Gibbs' 1930s Mediterranean-style home alert neighbors that he and partner Paco Argiz will be entertaining during the holidays. *Photography by Garry Chilluffo, courtesy Jamie Gibbs Associates*

In the entry, poinsettias and garland rope emphasize the drama of the gilded bronze staircase—showcase for a nutcracker collection. Antique dolls are arrayed on the nineteenth-century French canapé. On the wall are eighteenth- and nineteenth-century portraits on ivory and eighteenth-century *qouache* sketches. Sconces are from the New York City home of Billy Rose and Fannie Brice. Gibbs, left, and Argiz welcome guests. *Photograph of Gibbs and Argiz by Betsy Dustman*

tales of Christmases past, or just catching up on a year's worth of activities," Gibbs says. "Now I have a grandchild. Christmas is really for the young and young at heart.

"We are the hub for family and extended family gatherings. On Christmas Eve, family members from both sides gather at my house, together with a few close friends who are truly family. About forty gather for dinner, followed by midnight church services."

On Christmas Day, Gibbs and Argiz celebrate at home with out-of-town visitors, family, friends, and neighbors who drop in for a buffet and to watch Christmas movies. "For Christmas dinner, Paco and I provide turkey, beef and ham, a few side dishes, and desserts," he says. "The family brings nibbles, more sides, and more desserts. Paco was born in Cuba and is a gourmet cook, so in addition to traditional American Christmas fare, we have roast pork, black beans, yellow rice, plantains, and everyone's favorite—flan. After seventeen years of our blended Christmas traditions, people would be very upset if Paco didn't make his coconut flan. My mother was a lousy cook, but she knew how to bake. Growing up we would spend at least two days making

cream cheese cookies, pressing the dough into the shape of wreaths, trees, angels, and poinsettias. With their colorful sprinkles, these cookies are a must at my house. My sister and I continue the cookie-baking tradition, joined by our kids and grandchild."

Wreaths matching the doors are made from greens cut from the couple's country property. Indoor wreaths are artificial and decorated with glass balls, ribbons and other shiny accessories.

Gibbs says that he and Paco "go crazy" decorating all ten rooms on the first floor, including stairwells and hallways. The first floor's three fireplace mantels are dressed in lavish garlands, swags, candles, and figures. Stockings are traditionally hung in the media room where the couple spend Christmas morning. "On Christmas Eve, after everyone is asleep, we hang stockings for our house guests so they have a surprise from Santa when they awake," Gibbs says. "We have a small forest of potted plants that winter over in the living room and day room. These are festooned with white branches and live poinsettias."

Two or three large trees decorate the first floor, and smaller ones go in bedrooms. "To make house guests feel

at home, decorations that have special meaning for each guest are hung on the trees," Gibbs says. A flocked, Victorian-style tree in the library is hung with antique German glass ornaments and other decorations with family meaning. In the media room, a tree is decked in red, white, and gold, with hundreds of white lights.

"While most of the Christmas trees are traditional, a tree with LED strobe lights goes in our bedroom," he adds. "It isn't very pretty up close, but we place it in a large picture window overlooking the circular driveway, that can be seen from the street. It looks fantastic from outside."

Gibbs's favorite ornaments are nineteenth-century glass icicles, usually placed on the two big trees on the first floor. Three Christmas tree toppers are rotated in and out each year: a nineteenth-century porcelain angel, a vintage three-tier glass orb, and a Neapolitan angel.

With the decoration still up, the couple host a now-famous Three Kings Party to mark Epiphany on January 6 for as many as 200 guests. "Outdoor decorations disappear after Epiphany so the neighbors know we are done entertaining—for awhile," Gibbs laughs.

Duncan Phyfe chairs (c. nineteenth
century) surround the dining table
covered with Plumridge silk table squares.
Above the early-nineteenth-century
sideboard (one of a pair) hangs a
nineteenth-century Russian landscape. A
French chandelier from the same period
is lavishly decorated with greenery and
fruit. The table is set with Waterford
crystal and nineteenth-century German
red flash-glass stemware. Sterling flatware
(c. 1897) is Gorham's "Lancaster." The
epergne is nineteenth-century French
sterling. Egalitarian that he is, Gibbs
places porcelain plates by Bernardaud (a
premier French firm) on service plates
from Wal-Mart. The crackers (gifts for
guest to pop open) are from Costco.

Previous pages After a gut
renovation of the grand house, Gibbs
chose Hollywood regency style for the
living room, which seats thirty for
cocktails. In this half of the room (the
other half is a mirror image), a portrait
of actress Imperio Aragon (Paco's Aunt
Fifi Diaz) hangs on the mirrored wall
above the fireplace. The nineteenth-
century Neopolitan crèche is from
Gibbs's family. The Gorham sterling
silver punch bowl holds a white orchid.

The Christmas tree in the library is decorated with family-favorite ornaments dating from nineteenth century to the present. The nineteenth-century canapé is a mate to the one in the entry. Atop the Crossville porcelain tile floor is a nineteenth-century Aubusson rug.

The Iranian carpet creates a mood of merriment in the morning room. A central nineteenth-century table from Connecticut opens to seat twelve. Jamie calls the lavish arrangement surrounding the five-arm Wallace sterling "Grand Baroque" candelabra "stuff, but seasonally fun!" Behind the table, a greenery swag crowns a handsome desk by Baker.

Following pages An artificial fir tree stars in the media room, where Gibbs and Argiz say they really live. The artificial fir tree is decorated every year to complement the room and that year's dining table decorations Walls are paneled in white oak by William Sandringham. A pair of nineteenth-century wing chairs were made in Rising Sun, Indiana, by Cochran. The 1960s bar cart—one of a pair—is gilt brass. Overhead is a Waterford chandelier.

Uncle John helps Gates and Reese Lyle open their gifts.

At home with
John Lyle

New York, New York

In 1980, John Lyle left Jackson, Mississippi, and followed his destiny to New York City as a designer of uber-chic furnishings and interiors. But come Christmas, he treks south. "Our Lyle Christmases in Jackson are all about family, heritage, and tradition, with a bit of my eccentric nature (having been in New York for thirty-five years) thrown in," he says.

Lyle usually arrives in Jackson the week before Christmas. "My mom, Betty, has the tree up and the presents wrapped. It's up to me to pull the holiday together. I do the finishing touches for our big family celebration, which includes my mom and dad, my three brothers and my sister, and their families. The holidays are especially about the children," he says.

Lyle's long-time friend, Mississippi designer Marilyn Trainor Storey, joins the party, working with the Lyles on details from textiles to floral arrangements and table settings. "Every year we work with a different color scheme," he says. "This year, in keeping with that Mississippi boy Elvis's song, we decided to have our own 'Blue Christmas.' We even played the song while setting the table for Christmas Eve dinner."

His mother's extensive collection of ornaments and miniature Christmas trees and Santas looked elegant against the backdrop of furnishings—many designed by Lyle—in materials that include luxurious textiles, parchment, shagreen, and metals. "My family is my greatest design support, and I am lucky to have made many of the elements in their homes," he says.

For a recent Christmas, fresh flowers were in abundance. "Marilyn and I went wild with masses of white tulips," Lyle says. "We also used scads of blue ornaments for the real tree, together with gold and silver metallic elements including gilded manzanita. Of course, we enjoyed more than a few Blue Christmas martinis."

John Lyle and longtime friend, designer
Marilyn Trainor Storey, decorated Lyle's
mother's house, where they were all
"home for the holidays." The fifteen-
foot-long, shagreen-covered, waterfall-
style sofa table is by John Lyle Design.
*Photography by Amelia Paterson Studio
MJW, courtesy John Lyle Design*

Inspired by Elvis's "Blue Christmas,"
Lyle and Trainor created their own
vision of a Blue Christmas—in upbeat
Tiffany blue. Neutral-colored walls and
furnishings are the perfect backdrop for
blue accents.

Candlesticks accent the bleached-parchment "Elizabeth" cabinet (by John Lyle Design) in the dining room. Creamy white accessories add contrast, and large glittering stars hang gaily from the chandelier. A few pieces of Tiffany blue accent the demilune table.

Silver chargers hold clear glass
plates in a striking blue.

In the entry hallway, white tulips and white poinsettias welcome guests. The grand rococo mirror is decorated with a swag of greens and luxuriously furled blue ribbon.

Blue Christmas Martini

1 cup Mississippi Cathead vodka
1 cup white cranberry Juice
2 ounces blue curaçao
1 to 2 tablespoons fresh lime juice
ice cubes

In a large cocktail shaker, combine ingredients and ice. Shake it (like Elvis). Strain into chilled martini glasses and imbibe!

Lyle's Blue Christmas martinis highlight the theme.

In the living room, a mirrored cabinet holds elegantly dressed Santas, with the orange and marsala "monkey tree" painting as a stunning backdrop.

Dustin Van Fleet

Adel, Georgia

When Dustin Van Fleet says he is busy, believe him! The owner of Van der Fleet Design does residential design, staging, and historic restoration. He also designs rugs for his Van der Fleet Custom Rug Collection, as well as products for his Funk Living vintage store. In each of these niches, Christmas is the busiest time of year.

Van Fleet describes his style as "traditional with a funky twist." The evergreen wreath on his front door dazzles with gemstones, ornaments, ribbon, floral picks, and a double five-loop bow with long, elegant streamers. Inside, the mantel and tree also drip with glittery ornaments.

"Christmas is a busy time of year for me personally and professionally, so my tree is always artificial," he says. "I just don't have the clean-up time needed to install a live Christmas tree. On the night of Thanksgiving, we assembly the tree and trim it as a family."

Van Fleet's tree gets the full Funk Living treatment with piles of ornaments, ribbon, bows, floral picks, and pine cones. "Each year I try to incorporate my favorite ornaments in a new way so the tree looks fresh," he says. "I love to add polka dots, harlequin and chevron patterns, and other whimsical elements and colors."

His tree toppers are show-stoppers. "I spend a great deal of time, money, and effort to make a different tree topper every year," Van Fleet says. "Sometimes I make an angel, sometimes I gather floral picks, and other times I find items encrusted with gems and weave them into something custom."

Van Fleet's favorite part of Christmas is sharing family memories and traditions. "On Christmas Eve, my mother and I bake for hours to supply the entire family with fresh cookies, pies, cakes, and fudge," he says. "On Christmas Eve as children, we were allowed to open one present. I continue that tradition (as well as the tradition of setting out fresh milk and cookies for Santa). Christmas to me is not about receiving gifts. I love to give to less fortunate people. It's always special to see people light up when you give the gift of warmth, love, and respect."

Above Photograph by John D. Clayton

Dustin Van Fleet has time to decorate only one tree at his home, and it must be a "jaw dropper," he says. *Photographs by Dustin Van Fleet, courtesy Van der Fleet Design/FUNK Living*

He uses a single color—red—to create the stunning tree his family and friends expect every year.

Giftwrap plays up the tree's color theme.

Clove-studded oranges lend Christmas fragrance to the living room.

On the mantel, Van Fleet traditionally hangs two stockings—one for him and one for Santa!

Golden reindeer antlers are bejeweled with cranberry glass votive candle holders.

Pattern-conscious Van Fleet adds decorations and polka-dot ribbons—a favorite motif—to packages and a wreath at the door.

A custom-designed bright red chest
with whimsical harlequin-patterned top
(available from Van Fleet/FUNK
Living) is tailor-made for Christmas.

At home with
Howard Wiggins

Nashville, Tennessee

Howard Wiggins' dad was Grand Ole Opry star Little Roy Wiggins. But even as a youngster, the son had something in mind other than a music career. At sixteen he purchased his first antique, a Copeland bisque dog. Encouraged by his parents, he earned a degree from O'More Design College and opened his interior design business in 2005. After working on hundreds of homes, he noticed that clients tended to make the same decorating mistakes, regardless of taste. "What were they thinking?" he wondered. His popular book, *What Were You Thinking?*, helps readers avoid making costly decorating choices.

No two Christmases are alike at the Wiggins home. One Christmas, he hung **garlands adorned with sterling ornaments**; they were attached to small, upside-down wooden pyramids that he designed and installed three-and- a-half inches from the crown molding. The feature remained throughout the year as a molding detail.

Another year, he substituted the traditional evergreen tree with an asymmetrical, sculptural tree made of copper patina firmly fastened to the living room floor. Its copper branches reached the ceiling and spread across the recamier. The stark simplicity of the copper branches gave a sense of a barren tree in the winter, he says. Tiny LED fairy lights and sparkling crystal ornaments hung from the branches to create a magical feeling and evoke winter's chill. Another year, a garnet-encrusted crown of thorns hung wreath-like on the fireplace screen."

Yet Wiggins does have a few traditions. His living room mantel is set with Baccarat crystal throughout the year, so he adds only Baccarat crystal stars on the mantel at Christmas. For a recent Christmas, he commissioned a **three-dimensional contemporary** rendering of the Madonna and child by artist Bruce Matthews. The entryway featured a pair of terra-cotta urns with peacock feathers and pomegranates—

symbols of Christianity—and antique iron finials. At the base of the urns, he added a *globus cruciger*, a formal symbol of Christianity. At the opposite end of the entryway, on the staircase hung a stocking in the shape of Santa's boot crafted by artisan Kathleen Mullaney. "I have only one child, and our tradition is to hang a single stocking at the foot of the staircase," Wiggins says.

A table in front of snow-dusted windows in the breakfast room holds a taxidermied fawn. The table and sideboard are laden with beverages and desserts when he is entertaining. "I like to serve food and drinks in various parts of my home. This encourages guests to gather in small groups and talk with one another," he says.

A silk pillow spells out a holiday message.

Following page A custom copper-finish Christmas tree glitters behind an antique recamier.

The elegant stair railing is capped by lavish greenery and bedecked with votive lights. At the foot of the stair is an ornamental Christmas boot.

How do Howard and his family celebrate Christmas? "I invite friends and clients for an intimate gathering in my living room to encourage relaxed but lively conversation," he says. "A favorite gathering place is around the large, square travertine cocktail table that I designed. I enjoy presenting a variety of finger foods displayed on my collection of antique porcelain serving pieces. Having been born and raised in the South, I'm particularly drawn to the old Paris porcelain pieces used in many finely appointed local historic homes. Like a true Southerner, I pull out my cherished antique silver flatware and serving pieces to refine the setting. I collect and use a variety of different silver patterns and styles, with the porcelain for added flair. I always appoint my table first and then decide what I want to serve."

Wiggins has collected different types of ornaments throughout the years. "I have a fondness for sterling silver ornaments that is rooted in a family tradition," he says. "One was not allowed to sit at the formal dining room table, set with silver and china, until one was of a certain age. This rite of passage has always given me a sense of being a true Southern gentleman, and sterling silver is always incorporated into my Christmas décor and holiday entertaining." He searches for unique finds during his travels and at antique malls and America's Mart in Atlanta.

The season begins with Thanksgiving. "I put up my Christmas tree right after Thanksgiving because I like to start my holiday entertaining then and continue up to Christmas," Wiggins says. "I host several small parties before Christmas. Christmas Eve and Christmas Day are

devoted to my family. My wife and I spend an informal Christmas Eve at our son's home with other family members from out of town. Light snacks are served and we watch Christmas movies with our grandchildren. The adults exchange gifts on Christmas Eve. My wife and I return to our son's home Christmas morning for breakfast and to see what Santa Claus brought the grandchildren."

Wiggins dismantles his décor the day after Christmas. "I gently put away all Christmas items right after Christmas to give myself time to reflect on the passing year and to reminisce about Christmases past," he says. "I go through this same period of reflection when I pull ornaments out to decorate. One of my favorite memories is of my son helping me place the ornaments. He would kiss each one before we hung them."

Previous pages A taxidermied deer
adds a woodland feel to the breakfast
room. A Schoenbeck chandelier hangs
above the table, with its marble
Corinthian pedestal base. *Photograph
by Reid Rolls*

Opposite page A faux finish rattan
bed is hung with colorful, ornament-like
decorative glass votives.

A small angel graces the guest room.
Shedding light is a porcelain Marbro
lamp with a unique finial designed by
Howard using an eighteenth-century
gaming chip.

In the master bedroom, a deer lamp
sports a red lamp shade. The heroic
Chinese imperial yellow cloisonné vase is
one of a pair. An antique apothecary
chest faces an oriental bed made of
rosewood, teak, and ivory inlay.

Vintage ice skates hang on the faux finish
entry door, with its panels of terracotta
and gold piping.

Opposite page Antique ballroom chairs in the entry flank a pair of terra cotta urns with greenery. A sunburst mirror is applied to a rococo mirror.

Festive holiday foods are displayed on a travertine cocktail table designed by Howard. Above the fireplace hangs a painting by Bruce Matthews entitled *For The Love of Money*. The fireplace screen was created from an antique Belgian window grate.

Roses fill a gilded bronze centerpiece in the guest room. On the wall above it is a collection of coral cameos. The silver teapot belonged to Napoleon's niece, Princess Borghese.

A commissioned contemporary-style Madonna and Child portrait by Bruce Matthews hangs in the entry above a baroque bombe chest. On the chest, treasured objects include an Imari charger, Lalique vase, Tiffany candy dish, and an Italian marquetry music box.

A scalloped overdoor swag intertwined with red ribbon signifies that Christmas has arrived at the home of Jenny Lunney. Ellie, Wilco, and Kato welcome visitors. *Photograph by Jenny Lunney, courtesy Two Cherubs LLC*

At home with

Jenny Lunney

Collingswood, New Jersey

Jenny Lunney, a transplanted Texan, spent her early career working at a Philadelphia interior design firm for commercial clients such as Bristol-Myers Squibb and PricewaterhouseCoopers. Later, she worked for an architectural firm specializing in hospitals and research centers. But her true love is flea marketing and antiquing. Today, Lunney is an antiques dealer whose interior design work is "on request," helping clients incorporate their antiques purchases with existing furnishings.

Her career change followed a trip to Paris flea markets and warehouses, when she opened Two Cherubs Antiques in Collingswood, New Jersey, to sell her finds. Lunney closed that store but continues to shop Paris and the South of France and sells her goods at New Jersey and Texas flea markets.

Lunney, of course, decorates her own home—and never so enthusiastically as at Christmas. Outdoor décor includes wreaths on the windows, a stuffed felt snowman on the front door, and lighted garlands on the front porch. Indoors, Jenny hangs garlands on the stairs and drapes it around paired windows in the dining room. "There is a daybed in front of these windows where the dogs love to lie all day long," she says. More garland and lights on the mantel are paired with a small glass nativity—a gift from her sister. Lunney purchased her son's stockings and embellished them with trees and reindeer. Her own felt-and-sequins stocking was made by her sister, and Lunney found her husband Paul's stocking at an antiques store.

A fraser fir is brought home and decorated the weekend after Thanksgiving, and her favorite trimmings are antiques. "My mom always had antique beads on our Christmas tree, and I continue that tradition," Lunney says. "I find them at flea markets, and I also have some from my mom covered in glass glitter. I love all kinds of ornaments, especially old glass ornaments.

One from my mom is two angels climbing a ladder—this one always goes near the top of the tree. And I have a few old-fashioned glitter birds. Of course I have a large Texas cowboy ornament collection since I grew up in Texas and my sisters send me cowboy-themed ornaments all the time. We also have many old ornaments that my father-in-law found at auctions."

Like a true Texan, Lunney serves chili and tamales to extended family on Christmas Eve. "When my sister from Texas comes at Thanksgiving, she usually brings several dozen of our favorite tamales," she says. "When I was growing up we would have tamales made with venison from deer season. Now you can get almost any kind you want."

The giant fraser fir Christmas tree is decorated with antique beads—a tradition begun by Lunney's mother. Handmade stockings hang from the mantel of a massive, 108-year-old granite fireplace with wood-stove insert. Jenny's collection of ironstone pitchers holds greenery. The black bear head—trophy of an upstate New York hunt—wears a lighted garland. A tray of refreshments rests on the ottoman in front of the overstuffed leather sofa preferred by the men in the family. The TV hides in a French armoire opposite the sofas.

A French country chest top displays a rustic nativity scene discovered in Hershey, Pennsylvania. On the mirror is a wreath handcrafted by a friend.

The dining table, with a dramatic zebra rug cover, is set for one of many meals served during the holidays. Stacked mirrors in graduated sizes add height and importance to the elegant centerpiece of red roses in a silver bowl. A red rose, sprig of holly, and antique monogrammed French napkin give each place setting a scent and sense of the holiday season. Minton dinner plates belonged to Lunneys grandmother; the silver flatware was her mother's. Surrounding the table are carved mahogany dining chairs with tracery backs. Greenery crowns a mirror above a Louis XIV cane-backed settee and the top of a double buffet from Paris.

A farm table and a wing chair that belonged to Lunney's great-grandfather create a cozy breakfast spot. Below a rococo painted chandelier (c. 1920) from Avignon, France, an antique English pine cabinet cum kitchen counter (discovered in Philadelphia) adds country character to the contemporary kitchen. Fairy lights strung across the top of cabinets add sparkle. An old silver coffee pot adds elegance.

On the sideboard is an antique silver service (possibly from Tiffany) that belonged to Lunney's great-grandmother. Crystal nativity figures were a gift from Lunney's sister, Teresa.

At home with
Joe Ruggiero

Los Angeles, California

Those who love television shows featuring classically beautiful interiors might wistfully recall *Homes Across America* hosted by Joe Ruggiero. His composed presence and insightful comments made for satisfying viewing that is missing in home shows these days. Joe was a pioneer in bringing home design to network TV, watched by 84 million households. For nine years he was chief design consultant for PBS's *This Old House* and spent two years as a design correspondent on ABC's *Good Morning America*. He also hosted *The Living Magazine* for Lifetime Cable Network and ABC-TV's *Home Show.* In addition, his Idea Houses influenced an entire industry. Each room setting had a distinctive lifestyle theme and showcased products from dozens of companies in to-the-trade design centers nationwide.

Ruggiero now has his hands full with a collection of upholstered furniture for Miles Talbott, wood furniture for Gat Creek, throws for Textillery, out-

door furniture for Terra Furniture, all-weather wicker for Viro, and fabrics for Sunbrella.

Christmas finds Ruggiero at home with his wife, Barbara. "Our Christmas Day ritual is to attend church, and then Barbara and I celebrate at home," he says. Later, "we have Christmas dinner with good friends and our three children and grandchildren."

Decorations start with a wreath on the front gates. "Inside, we decorate the main living rooms and dining room. Sometimes we hang a wreath inside. We decorate windows differently from year to year. Last year, we used paper snowflakes made by the grandchildren. On the mantel we place a Hummel nativity scene."

There is one Christmas tree at the Ruggieros, always live and usually decorated traditionally. "We trim the tree with a combination of our grandchildren's homemade decorations and with things from nature," Ruggiero says. (Remember his wonderful book,

Found Objects? [Random House, 1988]) "Sometimes we add ornaments in exciting colors. And we like to change ornaments each year, using new decorations that our grandchildren have made. Our tree topper is a Swedish paper star that we have had for forty-six years."

A garden trellis is a handsome backdrop for vivid red poinsettias. Joe and Barbara Ruggiero love the fact that poinsettias thrive outdoors in California. *Photos courtesy Joe Ruggiero Designs*

Opposite page The couple likes to make each package special with papers, ribbons, and decorations they have collected.

A bowl of oranges—a traditional
symbol and fragrance of
Christmas—and ruby red goblets
decorate the long dining table set
for a family holiday meal.

Red ribbon and ruby glass evoke
Christmas in the gathering room.

Ruggiero shows us that red flowers do
not have to be poinsettias to say
Christmas. Red roses and carnations
mix happily with holly berries and
greenery in a centerpiece. The
Ruggieros collected the gold cachepots
on their travels.

An orchid is at home with red holly
berries and seasonal greenery. Ruggiero
believes that exotic orchids make
California Christmases festive.

A most unusual "Christmas tree" is
treated to a shimmering purple tree
topper.

Guarding the entrance, Leo makes a memorable first impression with his crown of evergreens and bowl of holly berries.

The Ruggieros spend time with grandchildren, who call them Grammy and Pop.

THE LAST WORD

At home with

Katharine Kay McMillan and David Strahan

We love Christmas in San Antonio

The weather is crisp but rarely cold, the vast blue sky is clear, the Hill Country is shrouded in subdued browns and greens, and the River Walk is lit up with a million gleaming lights. It is truly a magical time.

A few simple rituals make the season special. We start by creating a hand-drawn Christmas card. Previous cards have depicted a humble hacienda with a long twinkling star heralding the birth of Jesus, the cowboy magi traveling to see the Christ child, and Santa and reindeer flying over the Mission Concepción, one of the five World Heritage mission sites in the Alamo City. The missions are extraordinary places to visit and learn about life in San Antonio during the 1700s. We often take family and friends on a tour and buy them hand-made clay mission **ornaments for their trees** (missionsofsanantonio.org).

It seems as though we wait until nearly the last minute to start decorating for the holidays. We tend to keep things simple. Along with the traditional glass balls, garlands, and fairy lights, we hang our Fiesta medals on the tree. Even though the ten-day Fiesta San Antonio (fiesta-sa.org) celebration is months away in April, the colorful medals convey joy and evoke so many happy memories for us that we decided they belong on our tree. Why not?

Food is a major part of Christmas anywhere, and in San Antonio Christmas means tamales, a tasty concoction of masa (corn dough) surrounding a spicy mix of meat (or beans) wrapped in a corn husk. *Las Nuevas Tamaleras*, a play by Alicia Mena about a new generation taking up the ritual of tamale making, is often performed during the season. It's a must-see! We love to make a trip to Delicious Tamales (delicioustamales.com) and pick up an assortment of flavors. On Christmas morning, we wake up, treat ourselves to pan dulce (Mexican sweet bread), and make our award-winning com-[petition chili to serve over the tamales,

with no beans, of course. San Antonio is wonderful year-round, but our holiday menus make Christmas in this unique city a special delight.

—Katharine Kaye McMillan

Following pages The tree is adorned with medals from "Fiesta San Antonio" and traditional ornaments. Framing the window is a swag of gold flowers and greenery with sparkling lights, crafted by Katharine from "found garlands" from the Salvation Army. *Photograph by Sandor Gonzales.*

A ceremonial Chinese tea set recalls the military service of Strahan's father in the Pacific during WWII. Texas landscapes, painted by his grandfather, David Crockett Strahan, in the early twentieth century, are displayed on the walls.
Photograph by Sandor Gonzales

Iconic Texas structures—Mission San Juan Capistrano, a simple wooden church, and an adobe hut—and traditional symbols of Christmas announce the coming season in hand-drawn greeting cards by architect David Strahan. *Photographs by David Strahan*

Simple, natural decorations are often enough. Red berries on holly branches conjure the stark beauty of winter in South Texas. Stacks of Christmas books on a drop leaf table that belonged to Strahan's mother bring in brilliant hues of green and red. *Photograph by Sandor Gonzales*

A painting of the Texas State Capitol in Austin dominates the "man cave" den. Needlepoint stockings add a dose of holiday color. *Photograph by David Strahan*

Iconic Texas country scenes sketched by Strahan receive holiday sparkle. Red tapers add bold color to the glittering candelabra that makes a nest for a pair of gilded birds. The gilt-bracket shelf was a gift from Palm Beach designer Jack Fhillips. *Photograph by Sandor Gonzales*

On the coffee table is a stack of Christmas books co-authored by the designer in residence, Pat McMillan.

At home with

Patricia Hart McMillan

Although I love Christmas, I thought I was through with holiday decorating when my husband, George, and I moved to Texas almost a decade ago. I couldn't help noticing, however, that the neighborhood houses without lights looked so forlorn. So George and I dug out the big box, checked the bulbs, and up went our lights. Each year since, we are delighted to see more houses decorating outdoors—more lavishly, and earlier!

Our new ritual is eating Christmas dinner out, and it's so much fun. I've never enjoyed cooking. (Is there an *I Hate To Cook* cookbook?) So our first Christmas dinner in San Antonio was at Mi Tierra. A sprawling family restaurant in the heart of historic downtown, it is admittedly a tourist attraction, but far from a trap. Open twenty-four hours a day year-round, it always has a line of eager diners. There's a huge, gaily decorated bar, a big bakery, and meandering seating areas with walls serving as brilliantly painted murals featuring notable citizens past and

present. (Anyone who is anybody is in a mural!) The décor is beyond extravagant, so anything I might do at home will always seem austere by comparison. We all love Mi Tierra. It's an annual *must*!

Of course, we do have meals at home, so I've begun collecting Christmas-themed dinnerware—casual, of course. And I set the table differently for each meal to heighten the sense of festivity. I have become a flea market fancier. While I never had time for that before moving to San Antonio, now George and I drop into a Goodwill almost weekly. I was delighted to be asked to design several vignettes for Goodwill's Christmas blog.

The holiday decorating is done by the time family members arrive from New York and Florida—except for one year when visiting daughter Leigh took up the challenge. She spotted a new, bigger, and better nine-foot tree for $60. Fantastic! I do love a bargain—whether it's from a to-the-trade-only showroom or Hobby Lobby, where Leigh found this tree. George was delighted that

Leigh assembled it and hung all the ornaments. Many of the ornaments were new. Some were from an unforgettably beautiful all-amber tree our late daughter Elizabeth decorated for her Palm Beach house years ago.

Recently we decided to downsize to more easily managed quarters, so we downsized Christmas decorations, too. We sent the tall tree and most of its decorations to Leigh in Florida. (I kept those with sentiment attached, like the ornament in its tiny gift box that designer Tina Lewis thoughtfully gave me.) In place of a big tree, we chose a tabletop tree that looks like a centerpiece. But I actually miss a tall tree and all the fuss involved in its decoration, so there will be a tall tree with all the trimmings at our new Hodgepodge Lodge.

Seeing the homes of designers on these pages has convinced me that some things cannot be downsized, and Christmas is one of them!

—Patricia Hart McMillan

The drop leaf dining table (from Mersman Waldron's Comfortables collection) is set for a holiday breakfast. Dinnerware, a gift from late daughter Liz Hart McMillan, is blue-and-white porcelain from Haviland Limoges. Tumblers were a gift from son George purchased at the US Embassy in Iraq. The Haviland teapot holds fresh holly branches and sports a red-and-white gingham ribbon bow. Chair slip seats, covered in leopard-print fabric in the early 1990s, still look fashionably new.

Opposite page A glass-front cabinet with pagoda bonnet (discovered in the mid-1980s at the Salvation Army store in Newark, New Jersey) displays a collection of blue-and-white jars and bowls. Porcelain figurines from a nativity scene were a find at the neighborhood Goodwill store.
Photography by Sandor Gonzalez

The table in the breakfast area is covered with a Burberry-inspired patterned sheet from Wal-Mart. The tabletop Christmas tree centerpiece is from Pier I Imports. The loveseat—a favorite spot for recipe reading—was purchased on a hurried late-afternoon shopping trip to 41 Madison (New York City's to-the-trade furniture building) for Liz's brownstone. It next resided in East Hampton before ending up in San Antonio.

Nutcracker figures discovered at the local Walgreen's are placed on pedestals flanking the gas fireplace. A garland spanning the fireplace is trimmed with red bows and streamers. The soft-sculpture red Christmas tree on the mantel is actually a door stopper. The tall chrome lamp beside the TV (one of a pair) is a Richard Tutching design from his Bridgehampton, New York, shop. On the coffee table is a stack of Christmas books co-authored by the designer in residence, Pat McMillan.

Ornaments hung on bare branches and a
Santa plate on a stand add a seasonal
note.

Mix-and-match china create a cheerful
table setting designed for the San
Antonio Goodwill blog. All items on the
table, except Pat's antique Fostoria
stemware, were purchased at a Goodwill
store for about $35 and illustrate a
favorite Pat McMillan maxim that fun
design can be inexpensive. *Photograph by
David Strahan*

In the library, Pat and George admire a
holiday flower arrangement from
daughter Leigh. *Photograph by Kat
McMillan*